THE
COLD WAR
IS
OVER

THE
COLD WAR
IS
OVER

═══════

WILLIAM G. HYLAND

T I M E S   BOOKS

R A N D O M   H O U S E

Copyright © 1990 by William G. Hyland
All rights reserved under International and
Pan-American Copyright Conventions. Published in the
United States by Random House, Inc., New York, and
simultaneously in Canada by Random House of Canada
Limited, Toronto.

Library of Congress Cataloging-in-Publication Data
Hyland, William G.
The cold war is over / by William G. Hyland.
p.   cm.
Includes bibliographical references.
ISBN 0–8129–1871–1
1. Cold War.   2. United States—Foreign
relations—Soviet Union.   3. Soviet Union—Foreign
relations—United States.   4. United States—Foreign
relations—1945–   5. Soviet Union—Foreign
relations—1945–   I. Title.
E183.8.S65H92   1990
327.73047—dc20   89–20638

Book design by Jenny Vandeventer
Manufactured in the United States of America
98765432   24689753   23456789
First Edition

For Evelyn

PREFACE

I joined the ranks of the cold war in October 1954, at the Central Intelligence Agency, then housed in an old wartime wooden building where the Kennedy Center for the Performing Arts now stands. The phrase "cold war" (believed to have been invented by Walter Lippmann) was already widely used. There was considerable pessimism about it. I do not remember anyone claiming that we were winning, and many in Washington were wringing their hands fearing that we were losing, or at least falling dangerously behind. There was a growing perception of a nearly invincible Soviet Union. This was always puzzling to the analysts who knew the Soviet system's basic weaknesses.

Stalin had been dead for over a year when I came to Washington, but his influence could still be felt. There was a popular CIA training course lecture provocatively entitled "Stalin's Organ." The thesis was that international communism was like a giant pipe organ, which Stalin played masterfully, pulling out various stops, changing tone and timbre and orchestrating the communist conspiracy. There was an inordinate interest in every tiny communist party anywhere, but more important was the widespread view that international communism was monolithic. Any dispute could be explained as merely a family quarrel—a viewpoint that proved to be dead wrong, but was extremely difficult to overcome even as the Sino-Soviet clash became more obvious.

Stalin's successors were fascinating objects of study. Who were they really? Were they still Stalinists? Was Georgii Malenkov's new course genuine, or a tactic? Were they reducing their army, spending more on consumer goods, and reforming the economy, as they proclaimed? Or were these temporary tactics? Would Malenkov defeat the others (then he was believed to be the good guy and Nikita Khrushchev was the bad guy). There were long and detailed studies on all of these questions. My very small piece of this effort was to analyze the Soviet tank industry (tank as in armored divisions). What stuck in my mind was the revelation that well after the end of World War II, the Soviet Union had continued to produce a large number of tanks, some of which were captured in Korea. The production was impervious to events—the same numbers were turned out, whatever the political climate.

Later, I moved closer to the real cold war—as a Soviet analyst during the Berlin crises, the Cuban confrontation, Vietnam, and the invasion of Czechoslovakia. My main involvement as a participant, however, began in 1969, when I became a member of the National Security Council staff at the White House under Henry Kissinger. It was the period that became known as détente—a totally unexpected turn of events, but a critical break in the cold war. Détente was necessary to restore the credibility of American foreign policy after Vietnam. The opening to China was a stroke of genius that led to the agreements with the Soviet Union on Berlin and strategic arms control, which have proved far more durable than we expected at the time. Indeed, none of the practitioners of détente I knew believed that the millennium had arrived. Certainly no one was so rash as to believe that the cold war was over.

Throughout, the same question was invariably asked, a paraphrase of Walter Bedell Smith's famous questions to Stalin: What does Russia want, and how far is it going to go?

I have not been a participant since 1977. The inspiration for the pages that follow was the strange partnership between Ronald Reagan and Mikhail Gorbachev, and, above all, Gorbachev's startling revolution. At first I thought that it was naive to believe that the cold war was over—how many times were we going to go through this same debate, which had started when I came to Washington after Stalin's death? But since 1985 something fundamental has changed—mainly inside the Soviet Union, but in this country as well. When I finished most of this book in the summer of 1989 it was still debatable whether the cold war was over. When the Berlin Wall started to come down, everyone had agreed it was over.

What remains is to understand what it was about. Journalists are fond of citing what they call the "cold war mentality." It was always an irritating phrase, but it was impossible not to develop that mentality during the Korean War, or the Berlin blockade, or when the Wall went up in Berlin, or when the missiles were discovered in Cuba. These memories make it difficult to adjust to the post-cold-war world. But after the last fifty years, it is a welcome challenge.

ACKNOWLEDGMENTS

This book grew out of an earlier book, *Mortal Rivals,* a memoir of Soviet-American relations between 1969 and 1977. In writing that book I was struck by how often an issue could be traced back to the 1940s or 1950s—that is, to the cold war. For most of my colleagues in the government, the history of the cold war was something they had simply absorbed. Many could cite chapter and verse of Soviet or American behavior in an earlier crisis, or recall an arms control conference, the rivalries of the Politburo, and the intricacies of the Berlin agreements. And when the cold war seemed to be ending, they were properly skeptical, but given their sensitivity to history were also able to recognize what was genuinely new. Thus, I was inspired to try to write down one version of the cold war.

I was encouraged to write this short book by my family and especially my wife, who tolerated with some amusement my growing addiction to the computer/word processor, and showed the proper sympathy for consternation when a chapter disappeared in the computer's maw. I was also encouraged by two close friends: Strobe Talbott of *Time* magazine, who read an early draft and gave me his usual valuable advice; and Peter Grose, my colleague at *Foreign Affairs,* who prodded me to keep writing. Mae Benett of *Foreign Affairs* patiently pulled together, read, and corrected the diverse drafts. And Peter Osnos of Random House, who observed and wrote about many of the events in this book, was a patient and sympathetic editor, as he was for my earlier book. Finally, everyone at the

Council of Foreign Relations and Foreign Affairs was tolerant of my preoccupations. I am especially indebted to the Council for being included in a fascinating trip to Moscow to meet for over three hours with Mikhail Gorbachev.

—William G. Hyland

CONTENTS

CONTENTS

THE
COLD WAR
IS
OVER

INTRODUCTION

The cold war is over. The United States and its allies have won. There have been no formal declarations or surrender ceremonies. Nor will there be a grand peace conference. Nevertheless, the negotiations of the terms of peace have already begun. They were started by Ronald Reagan and Mikhail Gorbachev, and are being continued by George Bush.

As has happened after other, more conventional conflicts, the peace treaty finally settling the cold war may prove elusive. Clearly there is a truce, and in 1989 events began to overtake diplomacy. In Eastern Europe the old guard was suddenly and dramatically swept away by massive demonstrations and a popular uprising against communism. It was a genuine revolution reminiscent of 1848. It began in August in Poland, when the Soviet Union refused to intervene to prevent the formation of a noncommunist government. The message was loud and clear, and by Christmas 1989, communist rule had disappeared in all of the ancient Eastern European capitals behind the Iron Curtain. Even the Berlin Wall had become a relic. None of this would or could have happened without the support, if not encouragement, of the Soviet leader, Mikhail Gorbachev. Whatever happens next, the old days will not return.

═════

The cold war began in Europe. That is where the Soviet Union made its early gains after World War II. But that is also where the communist system failed most decisively. There were important battles in Asia, and had China not rebelled against Soviet hegemony, the outcome of the cold war might have been different. For a time there were important communist gains in outlying areas—in the Middle East, in Cuba, and in Africa. But in Eastern Europe, Stalin's empire could not nurture any enduring roots. Most of the governments were little more than puppets of Russian masters. And this empire was subjected to periodic shocks—in Hungary in 1956, Czechoslovakia in 1968, and Poland in 1981. Then in 1988–89 the entire structure began to disintegrate, even East Germany, supposedly a bastion of stability.

Throughout the cold war, the Soviet Union's various designs were sharply rebuffed and rejected in Western Europe. The western communist parties—especially in France and Italy—had emerged as potent factors after the war but gradually faded as Europe recovered. The Soviet Union's principal enemy, Germany, remained divided, but the western part was incorporated into a new anticommunist alliance and rearmed. In the end this new European alliance, as well as America's alliance with Japan in the Far East, counted most in the postwar balance. It became irrelevant to the outcome of the East-West struggle that a hapless dictator in Ghana or Ethiopia proclaimed fidelity to Marxism-Leninism. What mattered to the world at large was that forty years after the end of the war, Poland, Hungary, East Germany, Czechoslovakia, Bulgaria, and Romania repudiated that same bankrupt doctrine.

The Soviet Union might somehow have managed this disintegration, or even forestalled it, had the Soviet heartland itself remained strong and united. But the cold war exhausted the Soviet Union, materially, politically, and psychologically. It suffered defeats in geopolitical confrontations and in ideological crises within the communist world. On only one major front could it compete—in military power—and the staggering cost of that effort added to the exhaustion. Nuclear weapons, which made the USSR a superpower, were not usable, nor could they be translated into the leverage necessary to discipline Eastern Europe, conquer Afghanistan, or intimidate the nationalities that were beginning to rebel at home. Moscow had to sue for peace.

The cold war has ended, but some of the key issues will not simply fade away. The most urgent question is the future of Eastern Europe. Can there be an orderly transition to a new security system in Europe? Can Gorbachev, or any Russian leader, yield an empire that all of his predecessors fought for since the duchy of Muscovy? Will a new dictator arise in the Kremlin, who will intervene as Russian leaders have done in Eastern Europe for centuries? Or is it already too late? If it is, what is the role of a weakened Russian state no longer obsessed with expansion?

And what of the cold war alignments and alliances? What role will China play, and Japan, as the cold war ends and there is no longer a clear common enemy?

And what of Germany? Its unification now seems only a matter of time. Is a strong Germany and a weak Russia a recipe for another European disaster?

And, finally, will the United States have the wisdom to remain engaged in a world role, even as its domestic problems grow more urgent and demand more resources?

These are the questions that now confront George Bush and Mikhail Gorbachev and may well confront their successors. Within both countries there are political forces that are nostalgic for the cold war, for its seeming simplicity, its pristine clarity, and—yes—its drama and adventure. But history has passed them by. The cold war is over.

What the cold war was all about is the subject of this book, which also seeks to answer some of the related questions: who started it, whether it was unavoidable, and whether it could have been settled.

The cold war was Stalin's war. He started it in 1939, when he struck a devil's bargain with Adolf Hitler to destroy Poland, partition the Baltic and Eastern Europe, and unleash World War II. Whether he was Hitler's ally or the ally of Roosevelt and Churchill, Stalin's goal was the same: first of all, to dominate the area surrounding the Soviet Union and achieve such ancient Russian aims as control over the Turkish Straits and the Baltic. But Stalin also had more ambitious objectives—a relatively free hand in Eastern Europe and substantial, if not decisive, influence over Germany. These demands became the core issues of his cold war. Stalin's western allies refused to recognize his gains as Hitler's ally, and thus long before the infamous Yalta Conference, the seeds of the conflict over the postwar order in Europe had been sown.

After the war, had Stalin stopped at some point, even after the coup in Czechoslovakia in 1948, and consolidated his Eastern European empire he might have won the cold war, especially after the victory of the Chinese communists. But it was in Stalin's nature to press on, and he pressed too far—in Berlin and then in Korea. In the end, Stalin lost his cold war because his challenges created a severe backlash: he made it possible for the United States to revive and rearm West Germany and to conclude a security alliance with Japan. The fruits of victory of World War II eluded him.

Stalin's war had little to do with ideology, the attraction of communism, economic models, or the hearts and minds of people. It was a straightforward power struggle, and was confined to those areas within the range of the Red Army's artillery (as Stalin himself defined it). It may well have been the prelude to a hot war. At least that was Stalin's prediction to the Yugoslav communist leader Milovan Djilas: after twenty years, he said, "we'll have another go at it."

Could Stalin's war have been settled by negotiations? Probably not. At the summit in Teheran, in 1943, he told Roosevelt and Churchill that his "worst nightmare" was the eventual revival of Germany. There were hints before he died, however, that he might agree to a neutral Germany. And his successors seemed ambivalent about Germany's future, at least for a few months immediately after Stalin died in 1953. Sensing this uncertainty, Churchill wanted to probe the new Soviet leaders in a summit meeting, but his western colleagues resisted the idea because they believed the West was too weak. (Western weakness was a strange refrain throughout the cold war.) By the time Eisenhower came around to Churchill's view it was too late.

If the new Soviet leaders had toyed with the idea of giving up their half of Germany, at the Geneva summit in July 1955 they had reverted to the safer course of a divided Germany. In Geneva the successors to Roosevelt, Churchill, and Stalin sealed the division of Europe. That was painfully evident a year later when the West did nothing as the Soviet army crushed the Hungarian revolution in October 1956.

The failure to test Stalin's willingness to reach an accommodation over Germany in early 1952 or to sound out his successors after he died led to an enduring and recurring cold war myth—the lost opportunity to end the conflict at the peace table. This fear was revived by the advent of Mikhail Gorbachev: his policies of perestroika and glasnost loomed as a new strategic opportunity for the West. It was this concern over "ships passing in the night" that was cited by President Bush as the reason for his first informal summit with the Soviet leader in Malta.

The cold war we are more familiar with was inaugurated by Nikita Khrushchev (who is undergoing a posthumous rehabilitation in Moscow). Khrushchev saw far beyond Stalin's limited horizons. He envisioned a new global contest in which the USSR could enlist the former colonies in the third world as Russia's allies. And he tried to do just that, extending the Soviet Union's reach into distant regions, Cuba, the Congo, Indonesia—to the alarm of the western powers. He preached the victory of socialism over capitalism and the virtues of the Soviet economic model; he expanded the concept of socialism to include some dubious candidates in the third world and tried to reintegrate Tito into the socialist family. And most ominously, he turned the struggle into a nuclear contest when he introduced the threat of "rocket diplomacy" in 1956.

But Khrushchev, too, failed. First he weakened Stalin's empire by tearing down the dictator's reputation, which was the last shred of legitimacy for the Soviet satellites in Europe. Then he split the international communist movement altogether in his clashes with Mao. He continued Stalin's campaign to drive the United States out of Berlin and Germany. When that failed, in desperation he tried to upset the balance of power by a rash gamble in Cuba in October 1962. That adventure also failed— catastrophically. Khrushchev was humiliated and then deposed.

The missile crisis was Kennedy's finest hour, and the world's most dangerous moment. No one can say what the consequences would have been had Khrushchev prevailed and had the missiles remained in Cuba. Probably there would have been a war. Surely Khrushchev would have been encouraged to continue his forward policy against Berlin. The Cuban crisis has been reinterpreted many times, but it was exactly what it seemed at the time: an effort to overturn the balance of power. That was the strategic significance of Kennedy's resistance—that the United States would not acquiesce in such a strategic revolution, nor be defeated in a strategic showdown. That was the lesson of Cuba, and that is why it brought Khrushchev's cold war to an end.

=====

To be sure, the East-West contest continued, but its character changed. The division in the communist world widened at the very time when the United States became embroiled in the last anticommunist war in Vietnam. When that war proved unwinnable, and seemingly unending, the United States began to search for an honorable exit, which coincided with a further worsening of the clashes between Moscow and Peking. When Leonid Brezhnev proclaimed his doctrine of unlimited intervention to protect the gains of socialism, after invading Czechoslovakia in August 1968, he so alarmed the Chinese that the stage was set for the first major realignment of power in the cold war.

In effect, China joined the other side in the cold war. The United States could play the China card. Consequently, Moscow tried to block a deeper anti-Soviet realignment by accepting Nixon and Kissinger's terms for a détente: an honorable exit from Vietnam, a Berlin agreement, and a limit on strategic arms—all of which led to the first sustained relaxation of cold war tensions in 1972–75. This détente did not last, but it demonstrated that there was an alternative to confrontation.

Brezhnev, however, feared that détente was not producing the anticipated strategic benefits, but instead was leading to a new encirclement of the Soviet Union: by America, Europe, China, and Japan. Chinese-American relations were normalized by Carter; Japan and China signed a friendship treaty; Europe was requesting new American missiles. Afghanistan offered an opportunity to break out of this encirclement, in an area of great sensitivity to all of Russia's antagonists. With the Soviet Union driving toward the Persian Gulf, it suddenly seemed that the cold war was back in a far more dangerous form. But this was not to be, because, in fact, the Soviet Union was losing the cold war. The ideological battle, the economic competition, and the political contest had all turned against Moscow. Only Soviet military power remained, and that was proving exceedingly costly compared with the gains it brought.

In 1985 a revolution occurred in the Kremlin. A new generation came to power, in the person of Mikhail Gorbachev. Gorbachev not only revived détente but began to go well beyond it. Obviously, he acted out of desperation provoked by the crisis of communism that was spreading inside the Soviet Union and within Stalin's empire. Indeed, it was the very areas Stalin had seized—eastern Poland, the Baltic republics, and Moldavia—that were seething with nationalistic resentment. And, of course, the supreme irony was that fifty years after the Hitler-Stalin pact and the disappearance of the Polish state, Poland had a coalition government led by noncommunists—exactly what Roosevelt and Churchill had proposed to Stalin at Yalta.

Gorbachev recognized what Stalin, Khrushchev, and Brezhnev refused to concede: that the custodians of Soviet power could not win the cold war, and could afford to wage it only at the risk of losing the Russian heartland. He had to concede autonomy to the states of Eastern Europe, tolerate the end of the Berlin Wall, and preside over the disappearance of the Brezhnev generation of leaders in Europe as well as the repudiation of Brezhnev's doctrine—all to save the Soviet Union, which was also under assault from its national components.

In the late 1980s the two superpowers began to work out the terms for a peace treaty, even as the revolution in Eastern Europe and the national revolt in the USSR shape the post-cold-war world.

Perhaps the cold war might have been avoided had Stalin died in the 1930s, or even during World War II. At least the conduct of the conflict would have been greatly altered. The cold war that did in fact develop, however, was inherent in Stalin's paranoia and megalomania. But equally important, the cold war was also inherent in the system that Stalin built inside the USSR and tried to transplant in Eastern Europe. Neither Khrushchev nor Brezhnev could break free of Stalin's system, and preserving it drove them into unwise and dangerous policies. Thus, the conflict with the West may not truly end until Stalin's system is substantially dismantled. Gorbachev is doing just that inside the USSR, and it has all but vanished in Eastern Europe; for these reasons it is possible to assert that the cold war is indeed over.

Let us turn to its origins.

THE ORIGINS

The cold war began in Moscow—to be precise, in the early-morning hours of August 24, 1939, when Vyacheslav Molotov and Joachim von Ribbentrop signed a nonaggression treaty and a secret protocol that divided the Baltic, Poland, and parts of Romania between the USSR and the Third Reich. Within a week, World War II had begun, and within three weeks Poland had disappeared, and a week later Stalin began to collect his dividends. On September 25, he informed Berlin that he would soon "solve the problem of the Baltic countries."

For his part, Stalin gave Hitler a free hand to attack Poland, and he also provided a secure eastern flank so that Hitler could turn and attack France the following spring. Stalin, however, had shrewdly dodged the bullet of war, at least for a time. The inevitable European conflict would be a war among the capitalists, and not the anti-Bolshevik crusade which Stalin had feared after the bargain between Hitler and Chamberlain at Munich. Most important, Hitler's war created an unparalleled strategic opening to advance Soviet power.

The godfathers of the cold war were Adolf Hitler and Neville Chamberlain: Hitler for shattering the European order and making the advance of Russia possible, and Chamberlain not only for blindly trusting Hitler but also for stubbornly refusing to treat with Stalin for an early alliance.

The British defense is that Stalin never intended to join with them in the face of the threat from Hitler. Stalin's negotiations with the British and French that summer of 1939 were never really serious, they claim. Perhaps that is correct. Stalin's pact with Hitler was not inevitable, but after the Munich crisis Stalin's choices had drastically narrowed. Like most European statesmen he saw the war coming; he desperately wanted to avoid it, especially because for Russia it might have led to the nightmare of a two-front war with both Germany and Japan.

Had he chosen to do so, Stalin could have provoked a massive European confrontation before the conference between Chamberlain and Hitler at Munich, by taking a clear stand in support of his Czech ally. But it was not in Stalin's nature to be too far out in front if he risked being isolated. He had learned this bitter lesson in the Spanish Civil War, when the Soviet Union found itself the last supporter of the loyalists, and the only major power still confronting the Germans and Italians after the British and French backed away.

The fact is, however, that Stalin deliberately courted Hitler, secretly at first but more openly later. It was Stalin himself who gave Hitler the signal of readiness when he proclaimed to his party congress in March 1939 that he would not pull anyone's chestnuts out of the fire. The Nazi leaders rightly read this statement as an opening to Germany (an interpretation later confirmed to Ribbentrop by Molotov when they were chatting during the signing of the Hitler-Stalin pact).

Was Stalin wrong to ally himself with Hitler?

Soviet officials still argue that it was Chamberlain, not Stalin, who was not serious in 1939 when the British were negotiating in Moscow for an alliance: both the British and French only wanted the Russians to bear the brunt of Hitler's attack. Theoretically, Stalin could have chosen to fight, or to stand ready to do so. After all, Hitler did hesitate for a few days when he realized that the British would fight for Poland. Perhaps faced with the Russians as well he would have retreated. And even if he attacked Poland, after that brief campaign a German attack on Russia would not have been strong enough in September 1939 to push far into the Soviet Union. The famous Russian winter would have descended, and the following spring France and Britain presumably would have been in the war

THE COLD WAR IS OVER

facing much inferior German forces; perhaps the defeat of France might have been avoided. Of course, we can never know. But what Stalin did was to give Hitler two years to prepare for an attack on Russia (Operation Barbarossa) and to feed his war machine in the interim—a dangerous gamble.

Yet the pact with Hitler gave Stalin something he could never obtain from Britain, a relief from the Japanese threat to his eastern flank, which eased after August 1939. The Soviets credit this relief in the East to Japanese defeats on the battlefield by the Red Army. There is also little doubt, however, that the Japanese decided after the Hitler-Stalin pact to turn away from the Soviet front, to move south into Indochina, and eventually against Pearl Harbor.

Soviet leaders, including Gorbachev, argue that Stalin saved Russia. Perhaps he did, but the price was almost intolerably high—twenty million dead, and a vast destruction from which the Soviet Union has never really recovered. The compensation was a new empire in Eastern Europe. For Stalin that was sufficient, but it was a different story for his successors, who were condemned to constant intervention to prop up his new European domain.

Almost immediately after signing with Hitler, Stalin began to create this new empire, exploiting his new alliance to reverse the territorial losses of 1918–21. The western Ukraine (eastern Poland), Latvia, Estonia, Lithuania, and Bessarabia as well as a part of Finland were all incorporated into the Soviet Union. After he died, Stalin would be denounced, repudiated, and excoriated for his many crimes, but none of his successors— including Gorbachev—would attack the necessity for his alliance with Hitler, or indeed repudiate the territorial gains he made as Hitler's ally.

Fifty years later, however, these gains were in areas that proved to be the source of a nationalistic revolt against Soviet rule. The parliaments of the three Baltic republics voted to annul the Hitler-Stalin pact and the consequent absorption of their republics into the USSR. After denying it for fifty years, the Soviet leaders were finally forced to acknowledge, officially, the existence of the secret protocol, but they still argued that the "people" of the Baltic had "voted" to join Mother Russia. Only a few dissident voices among Soviet scholars raised questions about the morality of the entire shameful bargain, and, indeed, of all Soviet foreign policy in this period.

In Moldavia (Bessarabia), in 1989 there were violent public demonstrations and a strong nationalistic movement to replace Russian with Moldavian as the official language, and seek independence, including territories of Bessarabia incorporated into the Ukraine. In the western Ukraine there were demands to restore the Catholic (Uniate) Church; this was subsequently approved by Gorbachev after his meeting with the Pope in the Vatican in December 1989.

Recognition of these acquisitions was Stalin's initial demand of his new allies in the winter of 1941, after Hitler had finally turned on his loyal Soviet ally. The western powers, however, refused to recognize these gains. Long before Yalta, the cold war had become a conflict over the postwar political-territorial settlement in Europe. Indeed, for the next twenty years, this was the essence of the struggle for Europe.

———

The origins of Stalin's cold war thus are not to be found only in the records of the summit meetings at Teheran or Yalta, or even the last summit at Potsdam. The roots go back to the 1930s and the rise of Hitler. Until then the Soviet Union had been largely outside the mainstream of European politics, a pariah, the subject of occasional alarums and Red scares.

The Soviet Union did not even return to European diplomacy until 1922. Its return, however, set a disturbing pattern that would be repeated many times over the years.

The occasion was the Genoa Conference, called by the British and French to consider the economic reconstruction of Eastern and Central Europe. The new Soviet state was invited, because the Allied powers still were hoping to collect on the wartime and prewar debts, but also because they were impressed by Lenin's adoption of the more liberal New Economic Policy (NEP) and the abandonment of the harsh war communism. Lenin had little choice, but the NEP led to wild speculation that communism was finished in Russia, that liberalism was reviving, and that with a little help from abroad Russia would return to the "civilized family" of European powers. Even Winston Churchill claimed that the Soviet Union was so desperate for foreign assistance that the Bolsheviks would be ready to change their policies. In a theme that would periodically reappear for decades, the London *Times* declared that the communist experiment was "at an end." Lloyd George, the prime minister, told the House of Commons that Lenin "admits they have been wrong, he admits they have been beaten."

Therefore, Russia would be graciously granted terms for its readmission to the club: the Soviets would pay their prewar debts, of course, and give up hostile propaganda, and then agree to refrain from aggression against others. In this case, however, Moscow might collect some reparations from the Germans—this was hinted at by the western statesmen. Lenin swallowed these initial indignities, and a Soviet delegation traveled to Genoa, stopping first in Berlin to sound out the Germans on normalization of relations between the two powers. These talks in Berlin were unsuccessful, but they set off a wave of rumors in Europe about Soviet intentions. The two outcasts eventually surprised the other powers by a separate bargain signed at the nearby village of Rapallo—a name that would henceforth be periodically invoked to warn of secret Russian-German machinations.

The Rapallo agreement was simple: each party renounced claims against the other, thus relieving both of any new claims that might have been granted at Genoa. The western powers were surprised and chagrined. As a consequence the Soviets earned a reputation for deceit that would remain until the war if not beyond. This was particularly true among British Tories, including Neville Chamberlain's brother, Austen Chamberlain. One can only speculate whether this momentary triumph (and betrayal) at Rapallo led the younger Chamberlain to Munich sixteen years later.

While the shock of Rapallo added to the deep suspicion with which the new government in Moscow was regarded in Europe, the Soviet

Union had nevertheless gradually gained some respectability by the end of the 1920s. It profited from the relative international calm prior to the Great Depression and the rise of Hitler, and its rehabilitation involved no clear European security obligations. The French security system in Eastern Europe was constructed in the 1920s without Soviet assent, let alone participation. The French guarantees to most of Eastern Europe—which were soon to become crucial and dangerous—were not supported in Moscow. The Soviet orientation was still toward Germany and to the Comintern—until the rise of Hitler shattered this comfortable illusion.

———

Hitler brought Joseph Stalin increasingly into the center of Soviet foreign policy. The foreign minister after 1930 was Maxim Litvinov, who approached the threat of the Nazis as a textbook case: to be countered by a collective security system undergirded with bilateral alliances. Hence he supported the League of Nations and sought out Russia's old ally and Germany's natural enemy, the French. An alliance of sorts was concluded in 1935. Like most European statesmen, however, Litvinov greatly over-rated the strength of France and the willpower of Britain. He had greater faith in the British (his wife was English), but after Hitler marched into the Rhineland, Litvinov began to have doubts about the ability of the Europeans to join in any truly collective security policies.

For the most part Stalin left diplomacy to Litvinov. Stalin knew little of foreign countries; he had seldom traveled, except for brief trips for party meetings before the Revolution. And his relations with Litvinov were apparently cordial, even though in 1939 Litvinov was sacrificed as a gesture to Hitler. Litvinov was never bothered during the purges (al-though his deputy was executed). During the war he served briefly as ambassador to the United States. Why Stalin spared him when many of his generation were purged is another one of Stalin's mysterious quirks.

Stalin, however, had a better insight into European politics than Lit-vinov. He too overrated the French army; in 1940, after the fall of France, he complained that "at least they could have tried." Stalin, however, was suspicious of both London and Paris. He was badly prejudiced against the British because of their intervention in Russia in 1917–19—which he blamed on Churchill. In 1946, after Churchill's Iron Curtain speech, Stalin said to the American ambassador, "He's at it again." Stalin also blamed the French for intervening in the Russo-Polish war in 1921, when Stalin was the political commissar of that front. The Red Army was compelled to withdraw, yielding ground to a new Soviet border, much more favorable to Poland. Stalin never forgot, and he took his revenge in 1939 when the Red Army advanced well into Poland in collaboration with Hitler.

By the mid-1930s Stalin anticipated that there would be another European war. But he saw the struggle in less sentimental and ideological terms than many of his comrades. His aim was not to avert war, but to ensure that if war came it would be between the capitalist powers. Stalin had once said that Russia would make the "last move." He was not against alliances, but wary of military obligations. True, he ordered Soviet intervention in the Spanish Civil War; but this was consistent with his view that the capitalist powers should be assisted in fighting each other. The Spanish Civil War had the virtue of turning Hitler toward the West, rather than the East, and embroiling him with the British and French.

Stalin's wariness was also reflected in his qualified commitment to Czechoslovakia: Russia would act only if France acted, and the French obliged Stalin in the pre-Munich crisis of 1938 by never calling in his commitments to Prague. But most important, Stalin was determined to keep the line open to Germany. There was always an alternative foreign policy. While Litvinov worked for the support of the League of Nations, Stalin allowed two of his closest subordinates, Molotov and the rising star Andrei Zhdanov, to send contrary signals, especially through sources in the Communist International, signals that kept open a German option.

Stalin was always keenly aware of the impact of events abroad on his own personal power position. It may have been the decisive factor in his foreign policy.

As war drew nearer, he was caught up in a life-and-death struggle to purge the Soviet communist party. It was a struggle of his own making,

17

to be sure, but the fact is that many of his opponents favored the Litvinov policy of aggressive opposition to Germany. There is reason to believe that one aspect of Stalin's purges was to relieve internal pressures for a more active anti-German policy. In his intraparty conflicts Stalin's tactic was simple: to combine with one faction—say, Zinoviev and Kamenev—in order to defeat Trotsky, and then seek new allies (e.g., Bukharin) to turn against the original coalition. Divide and conquer was the essence. He was prepared to apply the maxim abroad: first to tempt Hitler by negotiating with the British and French but then to offer Hitler a secure frontier for his attack on Poland, and then to encourage his attack on France, and, above all, to take advantage of the interlude after the fall of Poland to make all the possible gains he could for the Soviet Union.

Stalin's major miscalculation was in anticipating that the capitalist war would be prolonged and would exhaust all the participants before it could ensnare the Soviet Union. This was the calculation, however, underlying his decision to ally with Hitler to the astonishment of the world.

———

Stalin's intentions were the source of never-ending speculation. Indeed, Stalin's capacity for surprising his friends and opponents never ceased.

Walter Bedell Smith's famous questions to Stalin—what does the Soviet Union want, and how far is Russia going to go?—were the eternal questions of the cold war.

It was Churchill who put the question more elegantly, in his famous phrase that described the Russians as "a riddle wrapped in an enigma"; but the second half of this quotation is usually overlooked, for Churchill added that the secret to the riddle was the Russian national interest. Yet determining what exactly was the Russian national interest was not that easy. When de Gaulle pondered the question of Soviet aims, he too saw it in terms of the traditional Russian national interest:

"To unite the Slavs, to overcome the Germans, to expand in Asia, to gain access to open seas—these were the dreams of Mother Russia, these were the despot's goals. Two conditions were essential to their realization to make Russia into a great modern, which is to say industrial, power and at the right moment to bring her into a world conflict. The first had been fulfilled, at the price of an unprecedented expenditure of human suffering and human loss. Stalin, when I saw him, was accomplishing the second in the midst of graves and rubble."

Despite their fairly realistic appraisal of Stalin's aims and methods, western statesmen could not quite believe that they were dealing with a true tyrant. Bedell Smith, for example, felt that Stalin's position was closer to a "chairman of the board" than outright dictator; Smith was no naive liberal but an old soldier, the former chief of staff to Eisenhower during the war. He was not alone, however. Eisenhower too thought that Stalin was limited by the Politburo; Averell Harriman and Harry Hopkins both believed that there were "sinister" forces behind Stalin. Even George Kennan, during the war, subscribed to the view that Stalin's powers were limited.

Inside the Soviet Union this attitude was summed up in the popular rationale "If Stalin only knew." This excuse for his excesses gave rise, outside the Soviet Union, to a belief that if only Stalin could be engaged personally, then all problems could somehow be settled. Truman was so convinced of this that at one point he explored a secret visit to Moscow by the Supreme Court justice Fred Vinson to contact Stalin. Even during the war Churchill and Roosevelt were convinced that Stalin's subordinates—especially Molotov—must have been acting without Stalin's approval; hence their periodic appeals to the dictator for his personal intervention, and their preference for summit conferences with him. That Molotov would have the nerve to defy Stalin is almost too ludicrous to suggest, but it fit the image of "Uncle Joe."

The nuance required in diplomacy is not an attribute that comes naturally to Russians, and certainly not to Stalin. But he had an instinctive grasp of power politics, and a recognition of the limits of *Realpolitik*—characteristics that were often overlooked by the antagonists who imputed a demonic skill to his strategies.

During World War II, for example, Stalin, Churchill, and Eden were dining and discussing the diplomatic styles of various countries. When the conversation turned to the Soviet Union, Stalin commented, "Perhaps we Russians are not as simple as you think." The British leaders protested against this implied accusation, claiming that the Russians were indeed formidable. But then Stalin interjected that the truth was between the two comments: "[the Russians] were neither as simple as some thought nor as skillful as others believed."

Stalin was, above all, a Russian nationalist. He gloried in comparisons of himself to the great czars. When faced with the near-collapse of his regime in 1941, he invoked Great Russian patriotism to rally the population during the war. When victory was finally achieved he did not praise the triumph of communism, but in a remarkable address on V-J Day, he said:

"The defeat of the Russian troops in 1904 during the Russo-Japanese war left bitter memories in the minds of our people. It lay like a black stain on our country. Our people believed in and waited for the day when the Japanese would be defeated and the stain would be wiped out. We of the older generation waited for this day for forty years, and now this day has arrived."

═══

Though Stalin towered over his compatriots, until well into the 1930s he was not often accessible to foreign diplomats. He created a small sensation when he attended a farewell dinner for the departing American ambassador Joseph Davies. And when Joachim von Ribbentrop arrived in Moscow to conclude the Hitler-Stalin pact, he was surprised to be greeted by Stalin at the very first negotiating session.

After the war Stalin's personal role was reduced and he became more and more a remote, isolated figure. He had two serious illnesses and was afflicted with high blood pressure, but he came to suspect all doctors and at the end, shortly before he died, was being treated by an army veterinarian.

Stalin was sixty-four when the war ended in Europe. When he began to celebrate his seventieth birthday in December 1949, there was a great gathering of communist notables, including Mao Tse-tung, all paying homage to the Great Leader. The celebration lasted—in the pages of the Soviet press—until the day he died, over four years later. In these last years, however, Stalin became a lonely, morbid old man.

He had no family—at least no one he would allow to be close. His second wife had committed suicide in 1934; thereafter he lived alone. His older son by an earlier marriage died during the war, as a German prisoner after Stalin refused to exchange a German officer for him. His other son, Vasily, was a reprobate; Stalin promoted him to a general in the air force, but he was jailed soon after his father's death. In the 1930s, when she was young, his daughter Svetlana was close to her father, and later she tried to create a new relationship, but during the war Stalin pushed her aside. He showed an occasional interest in his grandchildren. He had an old housekeeper and a retinue of bodyguards and servants who attended him in his country dacha.

Stalin was a small man. This always surprised his visitors and western interlocutors, who expected a dominating physical presence, a big, impressive stature, the man of steel, with a large booming voice. In fact, he was short and stocky, "square and erect," as one visitor described him. His complexion was pockmarked, though this was not so noticeable as he grew older. Some remarked on his "sallow" complexion, others on his "oriental" features. His eyes were striking to visitors: "dark and flashing" was the usual description. He wore a simple soldier's uniform during the war, with no decorations, except occasionally the single gold star of a Hero of the Soviet Union. He was a constant pipe smoker, but before he died he gave up smoking, which no doubt added to his foul temper.

Most observers were struck by his quiet manner; he had a "genuine charm," according to Churchill's interpreter, and some even detected a sense of humor. He was a good listener, doodled constantly during a conversation, and spoke quietly but crisply and to the point. He generally dominated his meetings, even with such skilled practitioners as Roosevelt and Churchill. One of Churchill's foreign office aides, Alex Cadogan, wrote in his diary that at Yalta "the President flapped about, and the P.M. boomed, but Joe just sat taking it all in and being rather amused."

Russian linguists always noted his Georgian accent, but his Russian was proper and his style laconic. His memory was remarkable, and his command of the issues was equally impressive; he had a good knowledge of history, discoursing on one occasion on the Napoleonic wars to a depth impressive to his listener, Winston Churchill.

The impression he made on his various partners from the West, however, was of a man free of illusions, realistic but ruthlessly ambitious and, above all, deeply suspicious. De Gaulle found him "all strategy, stubborn and suspicious—possessed by a will to power." Anthony Eden saw Stalin more than most westerners. His first encounter with the Soviet dictator was in a long conversation in 1935. In his memoirs Eden wrote: "Though I knew the man to be a man without mercy, I respected the quality of his mind and even felt a sympathy which I have never been able entirely to analyze." Stalin was the "quietest dictator" Eden had ever known; "Yet the strength was there, unmistakably." Eden's later description was that Stalin was "prudent but ruthless." An apt summary.

After 1950, foreigners saw even less of Stalin than in the immediate postwar years, when he occasionally would intervene in meetings of foreign ministers. He gradually became addicted to a bizarre life-style, organized around his strange habits. He would arise in the afternoon, and begin reading and working; by late evening, he would depart for his nearby country dacha, perhaps for a movie (he greatly enjoyed movies, especially American westerns); often by early morning, around one o'clock, he would summon his colleagues for a supper. Then would begin an evening of drinking (pepper vodka), eating, and even singing and dancing; Stalin would man an old victrola, sometimes cranking it, while the others danced and sang. Occasionally Stalin would join the song and dance. Visitors would also be invited to some of these occasions, especially the foreign communist leaders. One of the Polish communist leaders found himself dancing with Molotov.

Stalin would finally retire to a small room where he slept on a plain cot. The room was sparsely furnished; there was an old table littered with packets of rubles, Stalin's pay from the Soviet government. Sometimes Stalin would hand a packet to Svetlana, for herself, or for his eldest son's little boy. The next day he would telephone his cronies of the night before; his failure to do so when he died was the first alarm that something was amiss, but none of his comrades had the courage to inquire for the entire day.

The Politburo seldom met. Instead there were the smaller groups, the "sextet" which made policy. The Central Committee was of no consequence, and there was no party congress between the last prewar congress in March 1939 and October 1952.

Politics continued, of course. But events took erratic, eerie turns. In the late 1940s there was the Leningrad case, in which most of the late Andrei Zhdanov's followers were purged. One of them, N. A. Vosnesensky, was shot; he had been a Politburo member and one of the regime's leading economic theoreticians. The Leningrad purge ran deep, and only narrowly missed the future premier, Alexei Kosygin, while claiming his brother-in-law.

After a lull of sorts, there was an even more bizarre event announced in late 1952: the so-called Doctors' Plot, in which a small group of doctors were accused of having poisoned some of the leaders of the past, including Zhdanov. It was pure fiction, and apparently arranged by Lavrenty Beria; to this day it is not clear what particular scheme Beria was hatching. Even Stalin was suspicious of the plot's authenticity, but apparently indulged Beria.

There is a serious analytical problem about Stalin that will probably never be resolved. He was a bloody dictator fully capable of ordering the death of millions, of instigating murders of his close colleagues (Kirov); he was a sadist who invited Bukharin to dinner the night before he was to be arrested. How did these traits, so well documented, fit with his image as a "quiet" dictator, capable of intelligent discourse and debate with the leaders of the world's great powers? Did these hideous personal characteristics influence his policies in the cold war, and if so, how?

Near the very end, Stalin began to turn on his oldest and closest comrades—Mikoyan, Molotov, and old Marshal Voroshilov. He accused them of being foreign agents, excluded them from the late suppers, and according to Khrushchev, intended to liquidate them. Only his death intervened to save them.

Aleksandr Solzhenitsyn has given us a fictional portrait of the aging dictator at this time:

"He was an old man without any friends. Nobody loved him, he believed in nothing and wanted nothing. Helpless fear overcame him as he sensed the dwindling memory, the failing mind. Loneliness crept over him like a paralysis. Death had already laid its hand on him, but he would not believe it."

STALIN'S WAR

Stalin knew what he wanted. In his negotiations with the Germans, Stalin was already establishing his postwar position. Most of what he secured from Hitler he retained, despite the opposition of his future allies, Churchill and Roosevelt. Both denounced his pact with Hitler and opposed his subsequent attack on Finland, his incorporation of the Baltic republics, and his pressures for territory in Eastern Europe. These conflicts were clear well before the western leaders began to deal with Stalin as an ally. They were the seeds of Soviet demands that would grow year by year until Stalin was in control of Europe to the Elbe.

Stalin's gains began with the fourth partition of Poland agreed to with Hitler in August 1939, which was elaborated in the secret protocol to the nonaggression treaty signed by Molotov and Ribbentrop. This protocol did not come to light until after the war, when the Allies located a copy in the German archives.

Poland disappeared as a political entity, and Stalin obtained about 77,000 square miles, an area reaching to Warsaw. In addition, the Baltic was secretly divided into spheres of influence: Estonia, Latvia, and Finland were assigned to the Soviet Union, and Lithuania to Hitler. Finally, Bessarabia, then part of Romania, was consigned to the USSR—Hitler declared his "disinterest."

Nevertheless, Stalin was uneasy. His claim to Poland had no legitimate basis. It was one thing in the eighteenth century for Catherine to tell Frederick the Great, "why don't we help ourselves" in the first partition of Poland. But Stalin believed he had to have some basis for retaining his gains. Thus, after the German attack on Poland, when the Soviet forces were scheduled to intervene to occupy their share, Stalin hesitated.

He waited until he could advance a public pretense for his actions, namely, that the Polish government had disintegrated and he was intervening to protect the "life and property of the population of the western Ukraine and western Byelorussia." The claims in this pretext, of course, irritated Hitler. Although the Germans complained about it, Stalin went further. In late September he reopened negotiations on the demarcation line, and in another secret protocol Stalin traded a part of Poland for a free hand in Lithuania. Hitler acceded, though this too heightened his suspicions of Soviet ambitions.

What Stalin achieved was alignment of his area of occupation in Poland roughly with the old Curzon line, established after World War I but swept aside after the Polish-Soviet war. Thus Stalin put himself in a position to argue at the end of the war that the Soviet-Polish boundary was a legitimate one, even though it incorporated substantial prewar Polish territory into Russia. The new line was also similar to the third partition line of 1795, but did include in the USSR the city of Lvov, which had never been Russian.

At this point—in 1939—the cold war battle over Poland began. The United States refused to recognize the partition. It issued a statement upholding the Stimson doctrine, that the United States would not recognize the acquisition of territory taken by conquest. Washington continued to recognize the government of Poland (then in Romania). The same pattern was repeated after Soviet incorporation of the Baltic republics, parts of Finland, and Bessarabia. None was recognized by the United States.

Stalin, however, considered retention of these acquisitions "absolutely axiomatic," he told Eden in December 1941. Moreover, he could cite some historical basis: the Baltic republics had been under Russian control for 150 years. And the new line in Finland established after the Winter War was about the same as Peter the Great's demarcation line. In Stalin's view, therefore, all of his demands were within the bounds of legitimate Soviet claims. He argued that parts of Finland were essential for the defense of Leningrad, and Bessarabia brought Soviet power to the mouth of the Danube.

If Stalin had rested his claims on security grounds, it is possible that Churchill and Roosevelt would have eventually acquiesced. Neither pressed their objections to the Baltic occupation very vigorously. And Stalin was permitted to accede to the Atlantic Charter in 1941. It is likely that Stalin expected that the Allies would give him the same free hand that Hitler had granted. Of course, he went well beyond his original demands to claim most of Eastern Europe. And that was his great mistake.

In this early period, Stalin displayed an iron discipline. Within days of the end of the brief Polish war, he insisted on mutual assistance treaties with the Baltic republics, moving Soviet troops into all three of the areas. Simultaneously, he began to press the Finns for concessions to improve the defense of Leningrad, namely, by obtaining a naval base and moving the frontier in Karelia farther from Leningrad. When the Finns refused, Stalin started the Winter War. This alarmed Hitler, but the bizarre turn was that the British and French began to make plans to intervene in Finland against the Soviets. Hitler's attack in France put an end to this folly.

Throughout, Stalin was sycophantic to Hitler, meeting his every demand. For a time even Hitler was intrigued by his new ally. So much so that during the Finnish Winter War, when Mussolini complained to Ribbentrop, he was treated to a lecture on the changes in Stalin, who had abandoned the Revolution and had become a sort of National Socialist, according to the Germans—an amazing theme that would echo in the remarks of various western statesmen during the war. In the end Stalin's appeasement did not sway Hitler, but it showed a single-mindedness on Stalin's part that bordered on the obsessive. Since his principal strategy was to buy time, he did placate Hitler by massive deliveries of material, but his determination to gain concessions in return was a harbinger of the way he would deal after the war.

―――

The remarkable consistency of Stalin's objectives was illustrated at three separate times: (1) in the fall of 1940 in conversations between Molotov and Hitler in Berlin; (2) a little more than a year later, in Moscow in December 1941, when the British foreign secretary, Anthony Eden, came to discuss with Stalin a treaty of alliance (this was also shortly after the attack on Pearl Harbor); and (3) three years later, in the fall of 1944 in Moscow, when Churchill confronted Stalin over the shape of the postwar world.

By late 1940 the Hitler-Stalin alliance was beginning to fray. There were growing quarrels over Finland and Romania, but Hitler had concluded a new pact with the Italians and Japanese, and he wanted Soviet adherence in some form. He proceeded to describe for Molotov a panorama of the world after his victory. The globe would be divided into spheres of influence, according to the Fuehrer. Japan would press southward to Indochina and Southeast Asia; Mussolini would move through North Africa, while Hitler would seek *Lebensraum* in "Central Africa." One assumes that this fanciful statement about Central Africa was invented to avoid the embarrassment of including Eastern Europe as the area for German *Lebensraum*.

In Hitler's grand scheme, the Soviet Union was then invited to "look toward" the Persian Gulf, and the Black Sea straits would also come under Soviet domination. It was meant to be a grandiose vision, but Hitler had not counted on V. M. Molotov, the man whom Lenin had called the Bolsheviks' best clerk. Molotov listened patiently to Hitler and Ribbentrop, but then bore down on such mundane questions as whether the spheres of influence in Europe allocated in the secret protocols were still valid. Stalin wanted Hitler's reassurance about the Soviet position in Finland and Romania; moreover, Molotov asked, what precisely was

Japan's Greater Asian Co-Prosperity Sphere? Where did Russia fit in? And what about Bulgaria? Hitler was evasive; he was seeking an Olympian dialogue and he was getting petty questions.

At one point in this discussion, Hitler let the cat out of the bag when he warned that the Reich would not tolerate a foreign power in Salonika. Why Salonika? Molotov asked. Hitler said because of the threat to the Romanian oil fields. Romania, of course, was being sought for the Soviet sphere by Stalin. Hitler had already made a mockery of the secret arrangement on Romania: after Stalin had occupied Bessarabia, Hitler invited Hungary and Bulgaria to take a share of Romania. Bessarabia was then incorporated into the USSR as the Moldavian Republic. (A footnote to history is that after the war Leonid Brezhnev, assisted by Konstantin Chernenko, took charge of this new republic.) Finally, Molotov was given a draft treaty to take back to Stalin when he departed on November 15, 1940. The secret protocol to the draft stated that the Soviet Union declared its "territorial aspirations center south of the national territory of the Soviet Union in the direction of the Indian Ocean."

The Soviets replied two weeks later, accepting the concept of the treaty, but proposing a set of conditions that are quite revealing of Soviet ambitions. The first was a reassertion of the Soviet Union's claim that Finland fell within its sphere. Second was a demand for a treaty with Bulgaria, including the creation of Soviet naval and air bases there, and situated so as to dominate the straits; Bulgaria was to be included in the Black Sea security zone, i.e., the sphere of the Soviet Union. Turkey would have to grant to the Soviet Union a long-term lease for "light naval and ground forces" to be stationed on the Bosporus and the Dardanelles. The third demand was that the "area south of Batum and Baku in the general direction of the Persian Gulf" would be recognized as the center of the aspirations of the Soviet Union. In addition, Japan would renounce its claims to the resources in north Sakhalin.

This ambitious list was presented on November 25, 1940, but there was never any formal German reply. Three weeks later, on December 18, Directive No. 21, Operation Barbarossa, was issued. It stated simply in its opening sentence: "The German Armed Forces must be prepared to crush Soviet Russia in quick campaign even before the conclusion of the war against England."

Had Stalin overplayed his hand? Was this an early example of the obsessive behavior that drove him to the cold war? Perhaps.

The new pressures for concessions in Bulgaria and Turkey were alarming to the Germans. It was a tactical error to insist on a lion's share in the Balkans. Hitler had conceded the Baltic and would have been forthcoming in Finland, but the new demands against Bulgaria and Turkey were red flags, so to speak. Nevertheless, Hitler was destined to attack Russia. His whole career pointed to that cataclysmic event—*Lebensraum,* the *Drang nach Osten,* the destruction of Bolshevism—these were the great themes of his life.

———

The scene changes. It is December 1941. Hitler's panzer divisions are within sight of the Kremlin; Leningrad is under siege; the Baltic republics are under German occupation, as is all of Poland. Romania has retaken Bessarabia, as Hitler's ally. German forces are driving deep into the Ukraine; the Soviet government has evacuated to Kuibyshev. Knowledgeable observers are predicting the fall of Stalin's regime. But Stalin has a new ally, the British Empire, which he had scorned so dismissively a year earlier. And the United States has entered the war. True to form, Stalin has already insisted on emergency military assistance and demanded the opening of a second front. It was in these circumstances that Anthony Eden arrived to begin a discussion of war aims and an Anglo-Soviet treaty of alliance. Stalin put on a bravura performance, insisting on British acquiescence in a series of postwar demands.

Stalin wanted a British guarantee of his gains under Hitler. He began by presenting a draft treaty of alliance, and proposed a secret protocol that called for: (1) transfer of East Prussia to Poland; (2) transfer of Tilsit and the territory north of the Niemen River to the new Lithuanian Soviet Republic; (3) reestablishment of Czechoslovakia with additional territory from Hungary; (4) reestablishment of Yugoslavia with the Italian islands in the Adriatic; (5) independence for Albania; (6) cession of the Dodecanese Islands to Turkey and rectification of the Bulgarian border at Bulgaria's expense; (7) reestablishment of prewar frontiers for all other powers, including Greece.

As for the USSR's western frontier, Finland and the Baltic "provinces" would return to their 1941 frontiers; the Curzon line would be the Polish-Soviet border; Bessarabia and Bukovina would return to the Soviet Union and in compensation Romania would receive Hungarian territory in the west. The Soviet Union would seek alliances with Romania and Finland that would allow stationing of Soviet troops.

Germany would have to pay reparations, and the Rhineland would be separated from "Prussia." Some sort of international military forces would have to be organized under the "democratic powers," which presumably included the Soviet Union. Eden demurred, for he was not authorized to discuss a detailed settlement, not even the Soviet frontiers, whereupon Stalin archly commented that if their war aims were different, "then there would be no alliance." It was an astounding statement considering the perilous situation confronting Stalin. And Britain, after all, had been fighting for over two years without a Soviet alliance.

Stalin persisted in a second conversation, insisting on the Soviet claim to the Baltic. Eden stood fast: Britain would not recognize changes in borders that occurred after the war began. Stalin accused Eden of following Chamberlain's line, predicting that the British would even claim that the Ukraine was not part of the USSR—an ironic statement by Stalin, who claimed at the end of the war that the Ukrainian Republic should be given separate membership in the United Nations.

Having taken a stand of principle, Eden then proceeded to undermine it by pointing out that the Baltic missions in London were not accepted as "representatives"; diplomatic notes from them were not accepted by the British government, nor did they have diplomatic status. Thus, the USSR was recognized as having de facto sovereignty over the Baltic. "A very curious situation," Stalin replied.

The Soviet leader went on to exclaim that the "whole war began because of these western frontiers. . . . That is really what the whole war is about, and what I would like to know is whether our ally, Great Britain, supports us in regaining these western frontiers." But Eden again begged off, this time citing a promise to the Americans not to agree to border settlements.

Eventually, Stalin hinted that his demands on Poland might be negotiable—"an open question"—but not his position in the Baltic states, Finland and Romania. The Curzon line might be adjustable, "but it is very important for us to know whether we shall have to fight at the Peace Conference in order to get our western frontiers." To which Eden replied, "I certainly hope not."

Churchill, who was in America at the time, wrote that "the time had not yet come to settle frontier questions which can only be resolved at the Peace Conference after we have won the war." The British government evaded confronting Stalin. When he returned to London, Eden argued that the British had to think about postwar collaboration with Russia against a revived Germany, especially since France would be critically weakened. Churchill appealed to Roosevelt, arguing that the Atlantic Charter ought not to be construed to "deny to Russia the frontiers she occupied when Germany attacked her." Churchill in particular feared that Stalin might even be contemplating a separate peace. Roosevelt took a strange position: if the Soviet army occupied the Baltic states, neither Britain nor America would "turn her out." Churchill, without waiting for this reply, however, had already reassured Stalin that he had urged Roosevelt to agree to "our signing the agreement with you about the frontiers of Russia at the end of the war."

Roosevelt summoned Litvinov (then ambassador to Washington) and told him that the United States would not oppose "legitimate" Soviet security. The British were miffed by this, and Eden in particular labeled Roosevelt's venture as a "dismal tale of clumsy diplomacy." It was during these exchanges in the spring of 1942 that Roosevelt sent Churchill a message including a statement that would haunt Roosevelt's memory: "I think I can personally handle Stalin better than your Foreign Office or my State Department. Stalin hates the guts of your top people. He thinks he likes me better and I hope he will continue to do so."

The president was not wrong. Stalin was suspicious of the British, and the "top people" in the British Foreign Office, some former appeasers, were bitterly anti-Soviet. But Stalin seemed to respect Churchill as a wily competitor who despite his anti-Bolshevism had supported an alliance with Russia against Hitler in the late 1930s. After the war, however, in 1946, Stalin complained bitterly about Churchill and revived the old charge that Churchill had instigated the allied intervention against Russia in 1919.

In any event, the British government signed a treaty, though without settling the boundary issues. Molotov accepted the treaty only after a talk in London with the American ambassador John Winant, who explained American reservations against any final border settlements.

Molotov was scheduled to travel to Washington from London and to discuss with both the British and the Americans the issue of a second front. By the spring of 1942 it was apparent in Moscow that the United States would soon be the dominant ally; thus placating the Americans was a prudent choice for Stalin. Moreover, it cost him little, for he ended with a new treaty with the British and an implicit commitment from both Churchill and Roosevelt that they would not challenge his border claims. Thus at the end of the negotiations in the late spring of 1942, Stalin had reason to believe that he had the support of the British and the implicit support of the Americans.

Eden's justification to the cabinet of the British position is worth recording, because it contained the kernel of the British rationale for a policy of further appeasement. He argued that if Great Britain wanted to remain a Great Power in Europe after the war, then "collaboration with a victorious USSR after the war will be essential," and Britain "cannot afford to neglect any opportunity of establishing intimate relations of confidence with Stalin." This of course was exactly what Stalin was counting on.

The Americans and British were relieved that the border settlement had been deferred, but their behavior had conveyed to Stalin a willingness to make concessions, and for the first time a difference in the approach of the Americans and the British. Thus there would be opportunities to play the Americans against the British. In any case, having ascended to one plateau of understanding, Stalin could raise his demands as his position improved during the war.

That these were safe assumptions for Stalin was confirmed almost two years later at the first summit, in Teheran in December 1943 (code name: Eureka). There Roosevelt drew Stalin aside for a very private meeting; he asked for Stalin's indulgence on the Polish and Baltic questions because of the coming American elections, but confirmed his acceptance of the Curzon line and the Baltic states in the Russian sphere. On the latter question Roosevelt said that once the Soviet army had occupied the Baltic states he did not intend to go to war on this point; in any case, he said to Stalin, the people would "vote" to stay with the Soviet Union *(sic)*.

Such utter cynicism of course had to be kept secret. Stalin only replied that he understood. The Poles were unaware of this conversation, as were the British. Both were shocked to learn of Roosevelt's private commitments when Molotov confronted them with a report of this conversation, during Churchill's visit to Moscow in October 1944. Churchill was not above needling the president when he learned of this indiscretion; he assured Roosevelt in a message that since the Russians wanted him to win the election it was unlikely that they would reveal his secret.

———

This visit of Churchill's to the Soviet Union in October 1944 is the third example of Stalin's pre-cold-war diplomacy. During this meeting the process of accommodation was carried much, much further. The issue of Eastern Europe, including Poland, was settled in fact, if not in name, after this negotiation between Churchill and Stalin. The popular myth is that the cold war began at the Yalta summit, in the Crimea in February 1945. Yalta was indeed an intriguing encounter for many reasons, including the interplay of personalities, but it did little to alter the basic strategic situation. The importance of Yalta is that the German question finally began to emerge. If the proximate cause of the cold war was Poland, the fundamental issue was Germany. During the war, both sides had reason to defer the German question, and to some degree both sides wanted to know about the final military lines before confronting the vexing problem of the postwar role of Germany.

When Churchill landed in Moscow in the fall of 1944, he was determined to settle Eastern Europe. At Teheran, he had chafed at the cumbersome formula of three-power talks; like Roosevelt he was persuaded that he could personally deal with Stalin. What he proposed to Stalin was breathtaking in its audacity: a partition of Eastern Europe and the Balkans into sharply defined spheres of influence. The Churchill formula began with Greece, which was to be 90 percent in the British (Allied) sphere, and in return Romania was to be 90 percent in the Soviet sphere; Yugoslavia would be in a gray area, with a 50–50 division of influence; the same formula was advanced by Churchill for Hungary, 50–50; but in Bulgaria the percentage was in the Soviet favor, 75–25 percent. This was written on a piece of paper, which the prime minister handed to Stalin, who simply checked it with a pencil and returned it. Within a few minutes much of what the world believed the war was about—democracy and self-determination—was swept away. It was an icy piece of politics.

Churchill surely did not believe that a 25 percent British interest in Bulgaria had any significance; it had no more meaning than the Soviet 10 percent interest in Greece. As for Yugoslavia, his formula was also something of a fraud. Although the Red Army was unlikely to reach there soon, Tito was becoming a dominant force, and he was a loyal Cominform agent—at least that was the perception of him at that time. The British had a vague hope of converting him from Soviet tutelage, but it was not a very realistic hope. Hungary, however, was an odd story; it was loyal to Hitler, but would almost certainly be invaded by the advancing Red Army. The British had no Tito ready for Hungary, and one assumes that Churchill's formula simply was a hedge against giving Stalin a free hand.

Czechoslovakia was never mentioned, but it was a safe assumption that after the betrayal of Munich, any Czech government would lean toward the Soviet Union.

Perhaps the most bizarre aspect of this cold-blooded deal was that Molotov spent two more days trying to shave percentage points off each formula, in order to get a slight edge in Yugoslavia (perhaps Stalin had sensed Tito's unreliability at that early date, but there is no evidence for this thesis). Molotov proposed to Eden that the Soviet percentage be raised to 75 percent in Hungary and 90 percent in Bulgaria; he then lowered the Soviet quota in Bulgaria to 75 percent, but raised the Yugoslav level to the same so that the Soviet influence would be 75 percent for all three countries: Bulgaria, Hungary, and Yugoslavia. Later he altered his position, which he then described as the "limit" of his concessions: Bulgaria at 75 percent and Yugoslavia at 60—i.e., a slight decrease from his previous offer, but obviously better than the Churchill-Stalin bargain.

And so it went. It is worth noting that the older issues now receded: the Baltic republics were not debated, for the Soviet army was already advancing into these territories; similarly the Finnish border was becoming moot; the Red Army was moving back to the Stalin frontiers. The immediate issue, already badly frayed by debate, was still Poland—not the old issue of the borders, but the composition of the government that would follow in the baggage train of the Red Army as it entered prewar Poland.

═══

It had been obvious in 1939 that if Poland was to be revived it would be under the auspices of one of the dictators, Hitler or Stalin. The Polish government in London had the support of Washington and London but little else, though a partisan force was subsequently built inside the country. No sooner had Hitler attacked Russia than Poland was reborn. Stalin asserted that Poland should be recreated in the boundaries set by Hitler and Stalin. Stalin, however, did not propose to recognize the Polish government in exile but to establish a new national committee—thus foreshadowing what he would do three years later.

The London Poles objected, of course, but at that early date, July 1941, they were subjected to the pressures of Churchill and Eden, and the pattern was established: British pressures on the Poles to make concessions to Stalin. Gradually Stalin prevailed. On the Polish issue his tougher, meaner streak began to emerge. His pursuit of the Baltic provinces and western recognition of his dominance in Finland and Romania reflected a quiet determination, an unyielding tenacity; yet it had no emotional content.

On Poland there was a difference; the discussions were often sharp and bitter. It became more and more obvious that Stalin had more in mind than drawing new borders; he would impose his political order on Poland. The break between the Polish provisional government in London and Stalin was precipitated by the German revelations in April 1943 of the discovery of a mass grave of Polish officers in the Katyn forest. The Poles in London accused the Russians; Moscow heatedly denied it, and broke relations.

The reaction to the Katyn affair became a grisly chapter. In effect, the Americans and British did nothing, even though it was increasingly clear to both governments that the Soviet Union was to blame. At the summit meeting in Teheran, Stalin even made a cruel joke about shooting German officers. Churchill was outraged at this obvious allusion to Katyn, but Roosevelt smoothed over the tensions. In August 1944, at the time of the Warsaw uprising, the Soviet army on the outskirts of the city did nothing to save the Poles. Churchill and Roosevelt were both puzzled, but no inquiry was made and no accusations were lodged.

These two terrible moral failures badly undermined the position of the western leaders with Stalin; he knew that they knew, and he sensed their weakness. He had an unerring instinct for exploiting moral cowardice, since it was his favorite tactic at home. (The Polish communist government finally revived the Katyn accusations in the summer of 1989. The Soviet response was to agree to an inconclusive investigation; some guarded admissions were published, but not an official acceptance of guilt.)

In any case, after the Katyn revelations and the break with the London Poles, Stalin had a free hand to organize the future Polish regime. Under pressure from Churchill and Roosevelt, Stalin agreed to renew contacts with the London Poles. But when Mikolajczyk, the Polish prime minister, arrived in Moscow in October 1944, he found that Stalin had already announced the formation of his own provisional Polish government, the so-called Lublin Poles, named for the place in Poland where their declaration was issued. Lublin was approximately on the Curzon line, thus emphasizing the new border. At Teheran, Stalin jokingly assured Churchill that he was not going to "swallow up" Poland. Now it looked as if he would. Mikolajczyk yielded on accepting the Curzon line, but it was too late. The British gave him no support, and he was discouraged to learn from Molotov that Roosevelt had betrayed him nine months earlier.

Thus when Churchill departed Moscow in October 1944, the postwar order was taking shape. Poland would be in the Soviet sphere in its new borders, with compensation at Germany's expense. This exchange of territory would virtually ensure that any Polish government would need Soviet protection against the revival of Germany. Romania was clearly in the Soviet orbit, and Bulgaria had been conceded. Hungary was still open, as was Yugoslavia, but Soviet predominance was likely in both. The western allies would be paramount in Greece, and in Italy, which was never really discussed. Czechoslovakia was already friendly to Moscow; in 1943, Stalin had worked out a modus vivendi with Eduard Beneš that gave the Soviet Union a virtual veto over major Czech decisions.

The fate of Eastern Europe was settled not by diplomacy or bargaining, or even slips of paper with crude percentages, but by the Red Army. Churchill knew it, probably as early as 1943, and Roosevelt knew it by Teheran in late 1943. It was Germany that was the major unsolved issue at Yalta—and for the next twenty-five years.

———

Churchill and Roosevelt both bear a heavy responsibility for the strategic outcome of the war in Europe. Having gone to war over Poland, in the end the British could not rescue it. Having betrayed the Czechs in 1938, in the end the betrayal could not be redeemed by either the British or the Americans. Having fought the war against fascism and Hitler, in the end much of Europe passed again under a dictatorship. A sad affair, but not easily avoidable without another war—or perhaps a cynical manipulation of the war, by permitting Hitler to fight in the East with minimal opposition in the West, a course never contemplated, despite Stalin's accusations to the contrary.

Given these frustrations, it is not surprising that the cold war was bitter.

Had Stalin behaved differently, the cold war might have been avoided. He was shrewd and even prudent; seldom reckless, and always tenacious and patient. Yet there was also a ruthless contempt for his opponents that drove him to excess. He invariably conducted his struggles at home in this manner; it was in his blood, and there was never any alternative in dealing with his opponents abroad. What Churchill and Roosevelt did not understand was that Stalin considered them not his allies but his adversaries. His contempt was scarcely concealed; in fact, on many occasions, especially with Churchill, it broke through in vicious personal comments.

It is Stalin, ruthlessness that causes observers to attack Roosevelt: that he was naive to believe he could ever convert Stalin. Yet Roosevelt was no fool. He was haunted by Wilson's failure after the Peace Conference at Versailles to secure Senate approval of the treaty and the League of Nations (Roosevelt had, after all, run as vice president in 1920 on a platform of supporting the League). The president was desperately concerned to preserve a modicum of goodwill through the end of the war, until the UN could begin its operation. That this was a utopian dream was not the issue for Roosevelt. That it could never succeed without the Soviet Union was the issue.

Churchill knew better, but he too was a prisoner of history. His nightmare was not much different from Roosevelt's—the 1930s, with the great power of the United States isolated from world events. Britain had to maintain the alliance with America, and to this end strategy, tactics, even pride had to be sacrificed. For this reason Churchill fares better than Roosevelt with the historians, and deservedly so.

Any judgment must take into account, and take into account heavily, the war itself. The dry and dusty documents cannot bring back those times.

Both men faced overwhelming problems. The American fleet was nearly destroyed at Pearl Harbor, and the war in the Pacific hung in the balance at least until the battle of the Coral Sea. Hitler had defeated the vaunted French army in a few weeks, driven the British off the continent, occupied all of Eastern Europe and most of European Russia and North Africa. His Japanese allies drove as far west as Burma, south to Indonesia, and almost to Australia. Much of China was under their control. That the two powers might even link up to India was not inconceivable.

Hitler's defeat was never foreordained. A small number of different decisions, especially during the first two years of the Russian campaign, and the war might have continued for years. The defeat of Russia would have freed the Japanese forces in Manchuria. The war had to overshadow everything for both Roosevelt and Churchill, and this gave Stalin a strong hand, particularly since he was not yet fighting against Japan. He exploited his position skillfully while the conflict raged. Once the war ended, his position was immediately strengthened, even though the atomic era had begun. While the western allies no longer needed him, at the same time their principal leverage—to stop fighting against Hitler—also disappeared. Moreover, the great wartime statesmen were also gone. Roosevelt was dead and Churchill was defeated at the polls. At Potsdam the Russian dictator sat opposite Harry Truman and Clement Attlee—both feisty and tenacious bulldogs; neither naive about Stalin or the communists, but not very knowledgeable. Both were caught in ending a war and returning their countries to peacetime.

Despite some very tough talk, especially from the neophyte Truman, who knew even less about Stalin than Roosevelt, the policy of Britain and America was to demobilize. As Roosevelt had predicted to Stalin, America was withdrawing from Europe: if there was to be another war, he had told Stalin, it would not be fought with American soldiers; Britain and France would have to do the fighting with American air support. The revival of France and Britain was questionable, and Germany was prostrate. Russia too had been profoundly wounded, but its army stood on the Elbe in a stronger, more advanced position than at any previous time in its history.

What is truly amazing is that what followed from 1945 to 1947 was not an immediate Russian advance but a pause. Despite the dire western warnings of Stalin's ambitions, sparked by the bitterness over Yalta, Stalin was cautious: there was no forward movement in Eastern Europe until the fall of 1947. He was also careful in Germany. He warned Tito about the risks in pursuing a civil war in Greece, and in the Far East the Chinese deliberately disregarded his advice to proceed slowly (the same was true in Indochina).

Nevertheless, the cold war began. It was more or less formally announced: by Stalin in a strident attack on the western allies in his speech of February 1946, and by Churchill at Fulton, Missouri, in his famous Iron Curtain speech in early March. But Stalin was not sure how it should be played. It is ironic that during the war, when the fate of his country was in the balance, Stalin displayed steel nerves (after a momentary lapse in June 1941) and played his cards brilliantly. With his survival and security achieved, however, he was uncertain how to proceed. So he waited.

BERLIN AND KOREA

Until the spring of 1947, Stalin moved cautiously. One reason was American possession of the atomic bomb. Truman had advised Stalin of that fact at Potsdam on July 24, 1945, but the dictator's immediate reaction seemed strangely indifferent: was he covering his surprise; did he already know the awful secret; did he perhaps not even understand? We now know that Stalin knew. Since early 1943 the Soviet government had had an atomic project, led by the physicist Igor Kurchatov. Marshal Zhukov in his memoirs records that immediately after Stalin's brief conversation with Truman, Zhukov, Stalin, and Molotov discussed Truman's news. Molotov commented that Kurchatov would have to hurry his work.

Nevertheless, Stalin did not seem to absorb fully what was happening to international politics, at least not enough to alter his view of the world. Like Truman, he was a pre-atomic statesman. His weapon was the artillery piece; where the Red Army advanced, that was where Soviet power followed; intercontinental warfare and global balances were vague theoretical exercises. When the Soviet Union had no atomic weapons and the United States had a complete monopoly, Stalin risked war in Europe by blockading Berlin. Even after the first Soviet explosion in August 1949, Stalin made no threats that even remotely smacked of atomic diplomacy. And he actually blocked any effort by Soviet military strategists to understand the changes in warfare that might be in the making as a result of the nuclear revolution.

Yet he recognized that the bomb gave the western allies a new card, and this reinforced his tendency after the war to tread warily until he could assess the geopolitical consequences of the bomb. Would the western powers still disband their armies as Roosevelt had predicted; would they withdraw from eastern Germany and Czechoslovakia, as they had promised in the agreement to divide Germany into specific occupation zones? Would the rough spheres of influence worked out with Churchill hold firm, or would the western powers challenge the Soviet Union's gains? Above all, what of Germany? Would it revive in fifteen years as Stalin predicted to Milovan Djilas in 1945; would the Soviet Union recover from the war and would they all have "another go at it," as Stalin also predicted? Was the postwar period beginning, or was it only an interlude before the contest would resume?

Stalin chose to wait, but when he learned of the Hiroshima explosion he convened a meeting of scientists and urged them to accelerate their work. "Provide us with atomic weapons in the shortest possible time," Stalin said. "The balance has been destroyed. Provide the bomb—it will remove a great danger from us." Yet he spoke little of the bomb in public, and when he did he was disparaging. It was to frighten people with weak nerves, Stalin remarked late in 1946 (thus foreshadowing Mao's more colorful description of the atomic bomb as a paper tiger).

But western possession of atomic weapons must have added to Stalin's instinctive caution. And he advised his new allies in Eastern Europe to act carefully.

Another reason for Stalin's hesitation in this early period was his experience in the Iranian confrontation with Truman. After the German attack on Russia, the British and Soviets agreed to put pressure on Iran to abandon its pro-German neutrality, especially since Iran formed an ideal corridor to send Allied supplies through to Russia. Soviet pressure was quite strong. In a note to Teheran of August 25, 1941, Moscow warned that the USSR would act on the basis of its 1921 treaty with Iran, which gave the Soviet Union a right of intervention. That note also stated that as soon as the danger passed, Soviet troops would be withdrawn. And about 100,000 Soviet forces did occupy northern Iran, as the British occupied the southern regions. Subsequently, the British, Iranians, and Russians concluded a treaty that called for Soviet withdrawal six months after the end of the war with Germany. The Soviets, however, had justified their intervention and their position in Iran on the basis of the older 1921 treaty—a right of intervention they have never renounced.

As late as the Potsdam Conference in July 1945 the Soviets pledged their support for the territorial integrity of Iran. But of course they did not withdraw, claiming that the six-month period began only after the end of the "war," which meant the war with Japan, even though at the time the Soviet Union was not at war with Japan. Moreover, the Soviets had already begun to put pressure on Iran for major oil concessions, which they wanted with or without withdrawal. The British were not eager to withdraw rapidly, but became alarmed about Soviet intentions: Churchill had warned Roosevelt in January 1945 that Iran "may be something of a test case."

And it did indeed become a test. Soviet aims soon became clear. A small puppet regime was established in Tabriz, called the Autonomous Republic of Azerbaijan. Soon thereafter a Kurdish People's Republic was also announced. Truman and his new secretary of state, James F. Byrnes, became alarmed and decided to take the issue to the UN—an action that outraged Stalin, who complained that Soviet troops remained because of a great danger of sabotage of the Iranian oil fields.

The date for Soviet withdrawal passed (March 2, 1946), but by then Moscow had opened negotiations with the Iranian government. Their demands were that Soviet forces remain in some parts of Iran for an indeterminate period, that the Iranians recognize the autonomy of the Azerbaijanian Republic and grant oil concessions to the Soviet Union. The United States meanwhile sent a note warning that Washington could not "remain indifferent" to a Soviet refusal to withdraw.

The Soviets concluded an agreement with the Iranians that included the oil concessions they had required and diplomatic recognition of Azerbaijan. Soviet withdrawal was completed by May 1946. The Iranians had

outmaneuvered the Soviets, however, because the parliamentary approval
required by the agreement was never completed. The Iranian government
meanwhile reoccupied Azerbaijan, the Kurdish Republic collapsed, and
communist ministers were forced out of the cabinet in Teheran. The
American ambassador reported that it was a "major victory for the UN."

The Iranian confrontation quickly entered the mythology of the cold
war as an early and outstanding example of strong resistance in the face
of Soviet probes. This was accurate as far as it went. But it was also
translated into a triumph of atomic coercion. That is almost certainly an
exaggeration. No atomic threat was ever made, and the whole issue of
Soviet withdrawal was on the table before Hiroshima (at both Yalta and
Postdam).

To be sure, Stalin was probing, but when he withdrew he thought that
he had in fact made major gains in the agreement with Iran; his two puppet
republics were supposedly guaranteed by that agreement. In effect he was
betrayed by the Iranian government of Amad Qavam. The outcome, in
any case, must have added to Stalin's growing frustration and irritation
with the complexities of postwar politics.

Meanwhile, in Eastern Europe Stalin was proving to be a poor em-
peror. As much as he admired the czars, he lacked their natural talent for
empire. Unlike the czars, he could not be the "Little Father" of his new
allies in Eastern Europe. He had conquered a conglomerate of nations,
some friendly, some hostile, a kaleidoscope of different political parties
and leaders, some under Soviet discipline, some autonomous; some occupied by the Red Army, some independent of direct Soviet power. It
would have taken the skill of a better imperialist than Stalin, who only
knew one system, the one that had succeeded in the Soviet Union: iron
discipline, supported by an ominous undercurrent of terror, punctuated by
occasional purges.

But transplanting that system to Eastern Europe during a postwar
détente was implausible. The western powers were still insisting on some
voice in the politics of the region, even to the point of inviting Czechoslovakia to join in the Marshall Plan in 1947. In Poland and Hungary there

were coalitions with noncommunists. Except for Yugoslavia, there were only a handful of communist party leaders in the area, most of whom had arrived in the baggage train of the Soviet army. (The East German communist leader Walter Ulbricht, for example, arrived on the outskirts of Berlin on April 30, 1945, a week before the surrender.) Few of these communist leaders had any standing in their own countries. Tito was a national hero of sorts, but he was also the leader least susceptible to Soviet authority. Soon it was apparent that Tito, acting together with the old Comintern agent Georgii Dimitrov, had startling ambitions, promoting the idea of a Balkan confederation.

To sort out this chaotic mess, Stalin turned to a subordinate who was rapidly rising in his hierarchy and had distinguished himself by conducting a sweeping and vicious attack on Soviet intellectuals and artists—Andrei Zhdanov. He was intelligent and talented, but ruthless and totally devoted to Stalin. He became the new favorite, edging out both Malenkov and Beria. For almost three years Zhdanov conducted a reign of intellectual terrorism, the Zhdanovshchina, a nationalistic, chauvinistic, and virulently anti-Semitic campaign. No one was spared; even Shostakovich wrote "An Ode to Stalin's Afforestation Program." Sergei Eisenstein, the famous movie director, was called in by Stalin and Zhdanov and instructed in some detail on the historical precedents for his epic motion picture *Ivan the Terrible*. (Stalin obviously relished comparisons between Ivan and himself, and went into great detail with the movie director and with Sergei Prokofiev, who wrote the score.)

If Zhdanov could revive Stalinism at home, perhaps he could apply the same draconian methods abroad. His instrument was the newly created Communist Information Bureau, the Cominform, successor to the infamous Comintern (Communist International), which had been abolished during the war. This new organ would provide Zhdanov and Stalin the slight cover they needed to convert Eastern Europe from a loose collection of semi-allies into a gigantic clone of the Soviet Union—all under the rubric of People's Democracies.

But there was a price for imposing this new discipline. It further alarmed the West. Nothing was more calculated to destroy the illusions of postwar cooperation than the creation of a successor to the dreaded Comintern. All talk that Stalin had lost his revolutionary zeal was suddenly vaporized by Zhdanov when he addressed the founding meeting of the Cominform in September 1947. Clearly, the Grand Alliance was dissolved. And to make it unmistakably clear, Zhdanov had revived the hoary idea of two hostile camps not only in Europe but in the world.

Stalin had already put heavy pressure on the Czechs to reject the Marshall Plan, and in his meeting with them (July 1947) he made it clear that the cold war was going to be waged with deadly seriousness. According to a Czech participant: "Stalin explained that the aim of the Soviet policy was to get the Americans out of Europe and Asia. . . . Czechoslovakia, which is an ally of the Soviet Union with the aim to prevent any resurrection of German aggressive power, cannot be both an ally of the Soviet Union and a participant in the Marshall Plan. It is a question of compatibility. . . .

"The interest of the Soviet Union and its allies, according to Stalin, is to force the United States to abandon its position in Europe and, step by step, in other parts of the world. Great Britain and France, if they have to rely on their own resources, are, according to Stalin, too weak to resist the interest of the Soviet Union and its allies."

The formal convocation of the Cominform in September 1947 ushered in a period of increasing hostility that had been reflected in these brutal remarks to the Czechs in July. As the French and Italian communists were removed or squeezed out of their respective governments, Stalin began to purge the noncommunists in Eastern Europe. The pressures began to accumulate. The break with Tito was coming to the surface. He was summoned to Moscow in February 1948, but refused to go; he sent Edvard Kardelj in his place, and Kardelj was given an ultimatum to coordinate all foreign policy with Moscow. He rejected it, and within a few weeks the whole dispute became public. The Czech government was overthrown in February 1948, and in March harassment began against the rail lines to Berlin. Real trouble was in the air. General Lucius Clay, the American

military governor of occupied Germany, sensed it even before the blockade, and he warned Washington that the basic threat was not to Berlin
but to the Allied position in Germany.

In early April, Clay wrote to General Omar Bradley, then chief of staff,
the following:

"Why are we in Europe? . . . We retreat from Berlin. After Berlin will
come western Germany. . . . If we mean to hold Europe against communism, we must not budge. We can take humiliation and pressure short of
war in Berlin without losing face. If we move, our position in Europe
is threatened."

By mid-June the Berlin blockade had begun. At long last the contest
for Germany was out in the open. The territorial issues—Poland, Romania, Finland—all were important, but Germany had become the heart
of the matter.

Stalin's attitude toward Germany was schizophrenic. On the one hand,
he hated and feared Germans. On the other hand, he admired their power
and wanted it tied to the Soviet Union. For most of the war his lust for
vengeance was dominant. In all important diplomatic dialogues he urged
breaking Germany as a European power: by dismemberment (one of
Stalin's favorite terms); by exacting heavy reparations to keep Germany
weak; and by transferring its territory to Poland and Czechoslovakia to
keep it encircled. These were for the most part visceral ideas; his proposals
went little further than generalized remarks—i.e., making Bavaria a separate state, as proposed to Eden in 1941, and detaching the Rhineland, or
four-power control of the Ruhr, were among his schemes.

These vague ideas were understandable when the Wehrmacht was deep
into the Soviet Union and Russia confronted the full force of German
power. Even as the war turned in Russia's favor, however, Stalin still
sought a weak Germany. Chip Bohlen, the astute American diplomat,
summed up Stalin's position in December 1943: "Germany is to be broken
up and kept broken up."

Roosevelt's ideas for Germany were not much clearer, except that his
geography was more detailed. He thought there might be three German

states north, south, and east; at Teheran in 1943 he elaborated further and devised more specific areas, including the Ruhr and the Saar. Churchill, on the other hand, thought that Prussia should be detached, but the rest of Germany could be part of a Danubian federation. Stalin became impatient with this small talk and said to Roosevelt and Churchill: "If Germany was to be dismembered, it should really be dismembered, and it was neither a question of the division of Germany into five or six states as [Roosevelt] had suggested. However, he preferred Roosevelt's plan to the suggestion of [Churchill]."

In front of his two wartime allies, he then delivered a few homilies about Germany. First, he said, there were no differences among Germans; they all fought like devils, except the Austrians. Therefore, the Prussian officers and staffs should be "eliminated," but as for the other Germans, i.e., Bavarians, there was no difference in areas. Second, a German confederation was artificial; it would only be the base for revival of a "great state," and there would always be a strong urge on the part of Germans to unite. As for Churchill's idea of uniting Germans with others (Hungarians), this was dangerous because it would only provide a larger framework for the Germans. Thus the purpose of a postwar international organization would be to prevent this tendency.

Stalin's conclusion was straightforward: "The victorious nations must have the strength to beat the Germans if they ever start on the path of a new war."

At the very end of this session at Teheran (December 1, 1943), Stalin provided another glimpse of his mental process: he proposed that the Soviet Union be given a small part of East Prussia, including Koenigsberg. This would not only provide an ice-free port but would also give Russia a "small piece of German territory which he felt was deserved."

As the war progressed and it became clear to Stalin that his armies would be in possession of large parts of Germany, he changed his mind. He became the champion of the Germans. A centralized government had to be set up and a final peace treaty negotiated. But he was careful in the postwar negotiations not to allow too much progress. He tried to buy

time, to consolidate communist control in his eastern zones, while prevent-
ing the same consolidation by the western powers in their zones of
Germany. He still wanted a weak Germany, and most of the clashes in
the four-power ministers' meetings were over reparations that the Soviets
were taking out of Germany without any accounting to their allies.
Stalin's efforts to extend his influence in the western zones was a delicate
operation, not exactly suited to Molotov's skills, or to Andrei Vishinsky,
the vicious prosecutor of the purge trials, who was becoming more and
more prominent in Soviet diplomacy.

What he wanted, Stalin told the British foreign secretary, Ernest Bevin,
in March 1947, was a centralization of power and decentralization of
administration. The western powers were not naive, and they understood
Stalin's game. Ambassador Bedell Smith in Moscow argued that rather
than fall into a "hollow" reunification of Germany, the West should
accept a further separation of the eastern from the western zones. And
indeed, this was what was happening. Soviet obstructionism was forcing
the West to revive its sections of Germany, and this worried Stalin more
and more.

He told George Marshall in April 1947 that he had no love, pity, or
sympathy for the Germans; while he wanted no strong central government, he was now opposed to dismemberment because it would be dangerous. Napoleon had counted on a divided Germany, which had helped
temporarily, but Napoleon had, in effect, given rise to Bismarck. Stalin
wanted a centralized economic authority, and this meant there would have
to be political unity.

What Stalin claimed he wanted was in fact being implemented in the
West, and the Soviets were mounting a campaign against it. The flavor
of the various talks with Moscow is best illustrated by the American
record of the very last meeting of the four foreign ministers in December
1947. The American record provides a small snapshot of Molotov's final
summing up:

"Molotov denied any responsibility for the impasse [at the talks] and
repeated earlier charges against the western powers. He accused Marshall

of asking for adjournment of the Council in order to give the U.S. a free hand to do as it pleased in its zone of Germany."

The failure of Molotov, or for that matter of Stalin, to slow down the slide toward western unification led to the Berlin blockade. That is the conventional wisdom. The blockade was widely believed at the time to be a gambit—an effort to put the western allies under pressure to negotiate a bargain for all of Germany. Yet it is also possible that Stalin saw it in cruder terms as well. After all, the western position in Berlin was severely exposed. There were only a few thousand soldiers stationed there, and without free access by land or rail the city would collapse. In other words, as Stalin had told the Czechs, he wanted to drive the Americans out step by step.

His gamble was dangerous, but for a moment it seemed that it might pay off. The Allied situation was in fact desperate, and few thought the position in Berlin could be held for more than a few weeks. Even as the airlift took shape it was regarded as a temporary expedient.

Truman made a fatal choice: he would not force the blockade on the ground, as General Clay urged, but try to negotiate with Stalin, and if that failed, try to stay in Berlin by some means or other. Even at this late date, Truman's position shows how much value was attached to contacting Stalin personally. A meeting of the American ambassador (Bedell Smith) with Stalin was arranged for August 3, 1948.

In this meeting and a later one on August 23, Stalin was "jovial" and restrained. His position was simple: the blockade would be lifted if the London discussions on setting up a German government were postponed; he did not want to force the western powers out of Berlin (he repeated this); he could even tolerate the fusion of the three western zones of Germany, but a German government established in the west would only be an embarrassment for the Soviet Union. In Berlin itself, the Soviets would issue a new currency for the entire city (thus assuring their death grip on the city's viability). Bedell Smith concluded that Stalin was eager for a settlement. Negotiations continued sporadically until mid-September, when they finally collapsed over the issue of Soviet currency for all of Berlin. Appeals to meet once again with Stalin were turned down; he was "on vacation."

These negotiations could have succeeded, and with some flexibility and skill the Soviets might even have stalled the formation of the Bonn government. But the Soviets were curiously clumsy and rigid. It was a time of some turmoil in Moscow; Andrei Zhdanov died in August, and by then Malenkov returned to prominence. Shortly after, a purge began of the former Zhdanovites. The split with Tito worsened. The blockade had begun as a clever strategy—it appeared that Stalin could not lose; if the western allies evacuated Berlin, their prestige would be permanently damaged in Germany; if they stayed in Berlin but gave up on the formation of a separate German government, they were inviting a Soviet-sponsored neutral government. But by early 1949, it appeared that neither would happen: the West was still in Berlin, supported by the dramatic airlift, and preparations for forming a West German government were proceeding. Far worse, the creation of the North Atlantic Alliance was moving ahead, and rapidly. Stalin was facing a major debacle.

One way out for Stalin was to put direct pressure on the Berlin airlift. But this was too risky. And it is an interesting sidelight of the Berlin crisis that at no point did the Soviets escalate. At the same time it was too late to devise a face-saving formula for a settlement. Stalin paid a high price in Berlin for his record of treachery since Yalta. No one in the West believed that he was serious in his desire for a settlement of the German question, and probably he was not.

For Moscow the division of Germany was not the worst outcome. Even though Stalin was contemptuous of the Germans as communists—communism in Germany was like putting a saddle on a cow, he once said—in the end, the division of Germany was tolerable. But he continued to try to weaken West Germany, hinting for some time at a bargain of lifting the blockade for suspension of western negotiations on a new West German government. It was a western inquiry about one of Stalin's public statements that eventually led to private talks between the two UN ambassadors Jacob Malik and Philip Jessup. Finally a formula was devised in which the Soviets simply capitulated and the blockade was lifted in May 1949—lifted, to be sure, without any new firm guarantee of continued western access. Nevertheless, it was a victory for the West. As General Clay wrote in his last dispatch from Germany, "Berlin had become a symbol throughout Europe of western determination to resist Communist expansion."

It was a stinging defeat for Stalin. But it was not Stalin's last offer on Germany; a few years later Stalin would make one more desperate effort to stop the realignment of Germany with the western powers, but by then he was already too late.

After Yalta, Stalin had forced the division of Europe, and the West eventually replied by dividing Germany and at least opening the door to its rearmament. Stalin had lectured the Czechs in 1947 that his strategy was to move the United States out of Europe, step by step. What he had achieved by late 1949 was the return of America in a new anti-Soviet alliance.

True, the Soviet Union finally acquired the bomb—the first explosion was August 29, 1949. It was much sooner than anticipated in the West, and sent shock waves throughout the world. Nevertheless, it was little compensation at the time.

———

In the winter of 1949, therefore, Stalin needed a victory, the more so because of the triumph of the Chinese communists. When Stalin's seventieth-birthday celebrations began in Moscow in December 1949, one of the more intriguing visitors was Mao Tse-tung, fresh from his victory over the forces of Chiang Kai-shek. His purpose in Moscow was not merely ceremonial. He was waiting on Stalin, applying for Soviet economic assistance and a treaty of alliance.

Stalin could not have been pleased. It is far more likely that he was alarmed. Mao was, after all, a living repudiation of Stalin's genius. For it was Stalin who warned against trying to defeat the Chinese nationalists, who counseled caution, just as he had done thirty years earlier when he virtually sold out the Chinese communists to Chiang Kai-shek. The breach had never been entirely repaired, especially since Stalin consistently favored other Chinese communist leaders over Mao. But Mao had won, and with minimal help from Stalin.

Nevertheless, Stalin exacted a high price for his support now that the war in China had ended. He insisted on retaining the Soviet naval base at Port Arthur. He retained other concessions inside China, including the use of the rail lines in Manchuria. In return he gave some economic help, supported by a small army of Soviet technicians. He signed in February 1950 a treaty of alliance that pledged the two communist countries to help each other if attacked by Japan, or Japan and an ally. (The treaty would be denounced by China in 1979, one year before its renewal.)

This was four months before the North Korean attack on the south. It is difficult to believe that the attack was never raised in their conversations. But the origin of the Korean war remains a mystery. It seems to have been Kim Il Sung's idea. Certainly Stalin had to approve, and may have even encouraged it. This is the version Khrushchev relates in his memoirs. Moreover, the Soviet advisers had created a well-trained and well-equipped North Korean army, as the Americans were to discover to their dismay.

Much has been made of American statements at the time that excluded Korea from the Asian defense perimeter of the United States. The most important statement was by Dean Acheson in January 1950, but this was not a sufficient interval to trigger an entire military campaign. And Stalin needed no such statements as an incentive; all American troops had withdrawn from Korea, leaving only a small assistance team. By Stalin's reasoning, Korea had therefore become an anachronism. As Berlin had seemed in 1948, Korea was in effect behind enemy lines—Stalin's line. If an attack succeeded, then China would have a small but successful rival on its flank, and if Ho Chi Minh was also successful, there would be two such rivals for Mao in Asia. Moreover, a small war in Korea would further inflame relations with the United States and block any American overtures to Mao.

Before the Korean War, Truman still had not decided to support the nationalists on Taiwan; some minimal link between Washington and the new regime on the mainland was still possible. Given Stalin's paranoia, it was sufficient that Mao had negotiated with the Americans, including George Marshall, after the war. Stalin turned out to be right—as a result of the Korean War, Sino-American hostility would continue for twenty-two years.

In any case, Stalin may have calculated that if the attack succeeded, without Chinese help, the Americans would be humiliated and the Japanese frightened. If so, the tentative Japanese peace treaty and mutual assistance treaty with the United States might be suspended or set aside. Just as the Berlin gambit had been aimed at a broader target of Germany, so Korea was aimed at Japan.

The Berlin blockade had been a major miscalculation, but a mistake within the framework of plausible analysis of objective reality—at least as Stalin conceived it. Berlin, after all, was quite vulnerable; and Korea was also vulnerable. But there was a world of difference between a limited thrust against Berlin, with an escape hatch still left ajar, and a frontal attack with mass armies. As a tactical military gamble Korea almost worked, but as a calculated strategy it turned into a monumental disaster.

Before the Korean War, the United States had begun to rearm, but without a sense of urgent alarm. Korea galvanized the United States. Thus in 1950, the defense budget that passed the Congress was about $13 billion; a month later, after the Korean attack, the Congress passed a supplemental bill adding another $11 billion, and then $17 billion more. The draft was increased and plans were made for an expansion of the armed forces from ten to eighteen army divisions; four were earmarked for Europe and began embarking in mid-1951.

Although it was not public knowledge, the Truman administration adopted a new policy document: NSC 68, which became the bible of the cold war. It had been completed before the Korean attack but laid aside for a time. In September 1950 it was formally adopted by the president. It portrayed a Soviet Union fanatically dedicated to the destruction of the free world, and proposed to meet it with a policy of global containment—a policy already well launched by the time the document itself caught up with events.

Stalin's response to the failure of Kim Il Sung's attack and the subsequent advance of American forces to the Yalu River line was to order (or encourage) the Chinese into the war. Tactically, this was a masterful stroke; it sent the Americans reeling back to the demarcation line between North and South Korea. Strategically, it was a more questionable and dangerous move. It added to western apprehensions that another world war was in the making. Many in the West feared a Soviet attack in Europe, perhaps against Tito.

If Stalin's principal aim had been to thwart any rapprochement between Washington and Peking, he succeeded. Otherwise the results were dismal. Japan was frightened, but frightened into the arms of the Americans. There was a huge American military force in Korea, not far from the borders of the Soviet Union. The American army was also returning to Europe in large numbers, four to five heavy divisions. Two new alliances were forming against the Soviet Union. It was only a matter of time before Russia's two wartime enemies would begin to rearm.

The time had come for a retreat, for regrouping, for a reappraisal of the new balance of power.

4

STALIN'S PEACE

The cold war took a decisive turn between the spring of 1952, when Stalin launched a "peace" offensive, and three years later, when a four-power summit meeting took place at Geneva in July 1955. Two important agreements were reached. Both sides implicitly agreed that Germany would not be reunited and that each side would consolidate and build up its sphere in Europe. It was also tacitly agreed that the two sides would not march inexorably toward a new war in Europe.

It began as a confusing period. Tensions over Korea were skyrocketing after the Chinese intervention in the war in November 1950. Washington was awash in official intelligence estimates and documents warning that a full-scale world war was not far off. The danger of such a war was the immediate apprehension of both Truman and Acheson when the National Security Council met after the massive Chinese attack. At the time, the Kremlin had been insisting that it would negotiate with the western powers over Germany, but this was widely regarded as merely a probe. Stalin's aim, according to a CIA estimate of December 1950, was to "break the will of the western powers to resist communist domination of Germany."

More ominously, a CIA national intelligence estimate (now declassified) stated that "there remains a possibility that the USSR may seize upon the present crisis to precipitate general war with the U.S." It was one of "the greatest dangers in [American] history," concluded a study by the

Joint Chiefs of Staff. The Chinese intervention was widely believed to be the forerunner of further aggression in both Asia and Europe.

China was acting as Russia's cat's-paw, it was argued. And as the combat turned against American forces, the debate began over whether to widen the war to Chinese territory. It was in this debate that Dean Acheson argued, at first almost single-handedly, that Korea was the wrong war against the wrong enemy. After Truman publicly hinted that the United States might use nuclear weapons in Korea, the British joined the debate. Clement Attlee, the British prime minister, flew to Washington in a near-panic to calm the situation. In effect he argued for a European strategy, concentrating on rebuilding Western Europe rather than bogging down on the Asian mainland. After a moment of panic, this was the position taken by the CIA director Walter Bedell Smith, the former ambassador to Moscow; he too saw Korea as a diversion to bleed the United States while Stalin proceeded to dominate Europe.

There were also other sober voices—especially those of the Sovietologists in the American government. Chip Bohlen, in a cogent memorandum in August 1951, argued that the Soviet Union's objective was not war, but preservation of its postwar gains. The Washington consensus, however, was that war with the Soviet Union had become inevitable, as laid down in communist doctrine, and that Soviet power was growing, while the West was only beginning to gather its forces. Hence the time was ripe for a Soviet-Chinese strike somewhere, and soon. And much of this atmosphere was conveyed to the Kremlin (perhaps even clandestinely by the British agents still operating for Moscow in Washington).

Bohlen was surely right. A war with the United States was the last thing Stalin wanted. And he began to take steps to defuse the tensions, especially as the Chinese offensive in Korea began to falter. And in any case, Stalin must have had some serious reservations about the Chinese. No doubt he encouraged—or perhaps even demanded—their intervention. But once the Americans had been checked in the north, as the war continued, control over world affairs in effect was passing to the decisions of the

Chinese general staff. Nevertheless, in this period there were no public hints of differences between the two communist powers. In the sharp Sino-Soviet polemics of later years, no attacks were made by either side about the conduct of the Korean War. There was only one note of bitterness, the Chinese accusation that the Soviets had charged rather high prices for the military equipment they supplied to Chinese forces.

Whatever Stalin's reservations about Peking, he began to soften his own position. First, he used an "interview" with *Pravda* in February 1951 to deny that a world war was inevitable, and he implied that the United States could easily stop the Korean War by negotiating a cease-fire with Peking. These were significant signals. The denial of the inevitability of war caught the attention of Washington. It was, after all, one of the cardinal tenets of Soviet doctrine that war was inevitable; the alternative of "peaceful coexistence" had not yet crept into Stalin's lexicon. Most Washington experts had long insisted that one reason the situation was so dangerous was this very belief in the inevitability of a final clash with capitalism, but now Stalin was denying it. Could this be a true change in policy? The Kremlin must have been aware of the strong political pressures in Washington to expand the war. Had Stalin recast the odds in a new calculation of the infamous "correlation of forces" which supposedly guided all communist strategy?

―――――

Stalin's interview preceded the failure of the Chinese spring offensives. Perhaps he anticipated that the Chinese military effort had run its course, as soon proved to be the case. Contacts were established with Jacob Malik, the Soviet representative at the UN, in late May, and formal negotiations were opened over a cease-fire in July 1951. The fighting continued, however, and it seems likely that Stalin was satisfied with a stalemate and may have preferred it to a quick settlement. It suited his interest to have the United States tied down in Korea. The Chinese, on the other hand, may have wanted to liquidate the conflict. Their behavior at the Kaesong and Panmunjom talks gave no early hint of their desire to settle, but their forces took a terrible punishment in the months of negotiating and fighting.

There were other Soviet moves in the direction of lowering tensions. In the fall of 1951, Andrei Vyshinsky, who had replaced Molotov as foreign minister, told the departing American ambassador that the two countries ought to prevent Korea from getting out of hand. And about this same time Stalin gave another interview, in which he played down the danger of an atomic war—significant because at that time the United States had just announced a new Soviet atomic test, the first since 1949.

None of this was particularly impressive to Washington, but it had some resonance in Europe, where fears of war had also grown after the Chinese intervention. Stalin had played on these fears and the desire for peace in his various machinations through the World Peace Council and the Stockholm peace appeal of 1950. Many Europeans feared that war would come, even if the powers wanted to prevent it. In particular, many feared that the revival of Germany would finally provoke Stalin. For this reason sentiment began to favor a new high-level meeting. One of the voices raised in this cause was that of the British opposition leader, Winston Churchill.

Before turning to European diplomacy, it must be noted that an important turning had been reached in the Korean crisis. The Europe-first viewpoint had prevailed. Generals Bradley and Marshall had finally supported Acheson. The United States would give priority to a buildup in Europe. And the war in Korea would remain limited and nonnuclear.

These decisions would force Stalin's hand. Western negotiations to end the occupation of West Germany were proceeding to a conclusion. Once it was agreed by Britain, France, and the United States, the western part of Germany would become a fully sovereign state. The West Germans themselves were deeply divided over this prospect—many on the left thought that this western alternative would mean the indefinite renuncia-

THE COLD WAR IS OVER

tion of unification. It was to this sentiment that Stalin turned in the spring of 1952, with the dispatch of his famous "peace note" of March 10, 1952. In it he tempted the Germans by evoking the great nightmare of Europe—a unified, neutral, but armed Germany.

This overture—sure to be rejected—suggested that Stalin was no longer as alarmed at the prospect of a separate German state; the imminence of a separate German entity might even widen the scope for Soviet maneuvers on the broader issue of European security. But a rearmed Germany allied with the United States was a different matter. Stalin always had a great respect for German military power, and his options were limited because he could not risk countering western rearmament by arming his own East Germans. So his peace note launched what had to be a political gamble: that the West would be too fearful of a neutral and united Germany, capable of maneuvering between East and West, and would thus, in the end, have to reject Stalin's offer and blame for Germany's division would shift to the West. Meanwhile, he probably calculated that his diplomacy would become a source of division in the West and especially in West Germany, perhaps even delaying Germany's integration into the western alliance system (Germany was not then a member of NATO).

This was the broad analysis adopted in western capitals, but the subsequent course of events has always been something of a mystery. In later years there developed in Germany a strong view that this brief interval was a "lost opportunity" for German unity. Was Stalin sincere? Would he have united Germany? After he died his immediate successors, Malenkov and Beria, were charged by Khrushchev with plotting to sell out East Germany; if so, the idea may have originated with Stalin. But this entire episode will have to remain one of the unsolved mysteries of the cold war.

At the time (spring 1952), Stalin's initiative did indeed prove divisive; the initial reply to Stalin's note by the three western powers was a counteroffer, to begin with free elections in Germany. It was clear that the western tactic was to gain enough time to ensure the signing of the agreements that would end the Allied occupation and grant West Germany full sovereignty. The signing of these agreements was scheduled for May 1952. Anthony Eden, who had become foreign secretary with the return of the conservatives to office in late 1951, had a feeling that there might be more than propaganda to Stalin's offer. But Acheson and Adenauer, and even Eden, finally agreed that the best approach was to avoid a flat rejection and to stall.

The Soviets persisted and began to make progress in dividing the western allies. Both Eden and the French foreign minister, Robert Schuman, decided that some form of four-power discussions had to be arranged if only after the agreements giving Bonn its sovereignty were completed. Acheson was "astonished" at the British and French, and Adenauer began to worry about a deal with the Soviets over his head. Stalin was not to be outmaneuvered, and despite stiffer western terms, he insisted on a four-power meeting, thus compounding the difficulties for Paris and London. In the end the diplomatic exchanges ran out of steam, and the Soviets stopped answering the western notes in the fall of 1952.

But Stalin's tactics had an impact. The official intelligence estimates, which had remained shrill even after the negotiations began in Korea, began to reflect a more sober tone. By late 1952, the CIA had reversed itself and concluded that the Soviet Union would not deliberately initiate a general war. Moreover, the policy planning papers in the NSC and State Department, largely under Bohlen's guidance, began to deemphasize the maniacal character of the Soviet regime. The avoidance of a general war and the preservation of Soviet power in the USSR became the dominant themes in these new assessments by the end of 1952.

For a brief period, George Kennan was the American ambassador in Moscow, and he added a keen analytical insight, suggesting that Stalin was not the madman portrayed in the earlier interpretations of 1950. Most intriguing was a new dimension: what would happen after Stalin departed. This became a real issue when it was announced in August 1952 that there would be a party congress in October, the first since 1939, and that the main reports would be given not by Stalin but by Georgi Malenkov and Nikita Khrushchev. Was Stalin preparing his own succession while still alive?

At this time, in late August, the French ambassador, Louis Joxe, had a brief interview with Stalin. He told Kennan the results, and Kennan reported:

"The French found Stalin showing his age very markedly. They said that his hair was noticeably thin compared to his pictures, his face shrunken, his stature much smaller than they had expected. They had the impression that he moved his left arm only with considerable difficulty and that his bodily movements were in general labored and jerky. They were struck by the continued brilliance and power of his eyes but felt that otherwise they were confronted by an old man."

The ambassador, incidentally, found Vyshinsky a "scared rabbit." Stalin warned the French ambassador of the dangers of the alliance between the United States and "Iceland." When the puzzled ambassador inquired whether the Great Dictator had meant U.S. air bases in Iceland, Stalin replied that he had meant Iceland's membership in NATO. Even Vyshinsky seemed surprised at this remark, but of course did not intervene (it was reminiscent of an incident several years earlier when Stalin adamantly insisted that Luxembourg was not one of the Benelux countries; none of his subordinates or his foreign guests cared to contradict him).

For Stalin the end was approaching, but he was capable of one last effort. First, his long, turgid theoretical treatise entitled *Economic Problems of Socialism in the USSR* was published. Supposedly it had been written early in 1952, but published in October for the education of the party congress. For the West, it was not without interest, because it refuted the notion that a war between capitalist and communist was inevitable, though the article allowed for new capitalist wars. Apparently it was meant to reassure the party faithful that Soviet policy was not bent on war—and that the international situation was not destined for a new war.

This new document by the master also created the framework for Stalin's successors to shift to "peaceful coexistence" as the new general line for the party. Whether this was Stalin's aim is not clear, but it seems a reasonable assumption that this document was the final step in a maneuver Stalin had begun in 1951, to pull back from the dangerous confrontation with the West.

Stalin also personally addressed the party congress in October, but very briefly. When he finished and encountered his colleagues backstage, he was ecstatic over his performance. "See, I've still got it," he exclaimed, as if a four-minute speech were a major accomplishment. Khrushchev, who relates this incident in his memoirs, was obviously contemptuous of the old man's pathetic behavior. But the next day the old master manipulator was not so pathetic. First, Stalin told a closed meeting of the Central Committee that he wanted to resign; this brought the anticipated protests and acclaim that, of course, persuaded him to stay. Whereupon he sprang a last surprise—he blithely announced a doubling of the number of members of the Politburo. The old-timers, including Khrushchev, were stunned; none had been warned and none knew who had fed Stalin the names of these new faces (among them Leonid Brezhnev). Of course, true to his style, Stalin quickly suggested that the business of the party be conducted by a smaller executive group, including Malenkov, Khrushchev, and Beria.

The post-Stalin order was beginning to take shape. But there was one last bewildering episode—the Doctors' Plot. Some Kremlin doctors were charged with having poisoned some of the leaders, including Andrei Zhdanov. No one knew what was afoot. The leaders suspected Beria. Stalin's daughter later wrote that Stalin was not fully aware of the accusations and had reason to doubt them. Before the plot could develop into a more elaborate campaign, Stalin died.

Shortly before, he had received the new Indian ambassador, who found him "robust and confident." In a passing remark Stalin had said that there were many good Americans but the system was driven by the thirst for

profits. Even though it was only small talk, it was Stalin's last pronounce-
ment on his main adversary. It was a pathetic summing-up.

Stalin dominated postwar politics. For most of the period his opponents
were on the defensive. After he died the initiative shifted first to his old
ally and adversary Winston Churchill, and then to the new president,
Dwight Eisenhower.

CHURCHILL'S
RETURN

5

There were two Winston Spencer Churchills. One was the British political leader, the champion of parliamentary democracy, the defender of freedom, the enemy of tyrants, and the wartime hero. The second Churchill was the successor to Palmerston and Disraeli—the prime minister who presided over the British Empire, who carefully managed the balance of European power, shifting Britain's weight to the weaker side, the sometime ally and sometime enemy of France, Germany, and Russia. It was this second Winston Churchill who returned to power in October 1951, more than six years after being turned out by the British electorate, at the very moment of his greatest triumph.

The man who returned to Number 10 Downing Street was much older than the lion of the 1930s who sounded the alarm against Hitler to no avail, or the coalition leader of the 1940s, who sounded the alarm against Stalin, or even the retired warrior who, at an obscure town in Missouri, had proclaimed the Iron Curtain and thereby accepted a certain responsibility for the cold war that followed. He turned seventy-seven a few weeks after his election victory but was still a formidable defender of British interests, the masterly orator who could turn the artful phrase, and a historian who could still grasp the broad sweep of the past and turn its lessons to the future. He had outlasted his allies and enemies. Hitler had been crushed, Roosevelt was dead, De Gaulle had retired; only Stalin remained.

Churchill was a heroic figure when heroism was no longer in fashion, but an imperialist with no empire. Nevertheless, he still thought in terms of grand strategy in an age of bureaucratic planning papers churned out in Washington and Whitehall. His grand alliance had won the war; now a new grand alliance, NATO, was a necessary bulwark against the East. But for him it was not a majestic undertaking. No one, he once said, would be apt to sing "March! NATO, March On." He had originated the idea of the European Defense Community, but as a grand coalition of great national armies; it had been turned into a "sludgy amalgam," he complained to General Eisenhower. Britain would not end its splendid isolation from Europe for this conglomeration, but would not oppose it either.

Churchill the statesman recognized that German power had to be summoned to balance the Russians. But he preferred a strong German national army. And he understood that this meant the French would look across the Channel for a guarantee; in the end this would have to come from the Americans, and then perhaps the British would join. British troops would stay in Europe as long as but no longer than the Americans, he told the French. He still believed in the balance of power:

"For four hundred years the foreign policy of England has been to oppose the strongest, most aggressive, most dominating power on the Continent. . . . we always took the harder course, joined with the less strong powers, made combination among them and thus defeated and frustrated the continental military tyrant whoever he was, whatever nation he led."

Yet he believed that Britain could no longer play that role. She was no longer powerful enough, nor was Europe strong enough, even with a German army: "We may be stronger," he said of the situation in late 1950, "but not strong enough in time to deter, still less to prevail." That could only be accomplished by the Americans. So he left the dreary business of negotiating the European Defense Community to Anthony Eden, but few were spared his lectures and acid commentaries. When, in 1954, the French Assembly finally rejected the EDC, Churchill commented he did not blame the French for killing it, but for inventing it.

What intrigued Churchill was not alliance-building but a grand settlement with Stalin. When he returned to office Churchill was in the process of finishing the last volume of his wartime memoirs, *Triumph and Tragedy*. And in 1953 he returned to the rewriting of a four-volume history of the English-speaking peoples. Both projects must have had a certain psychological effect on the new prime minister. In *Triumph and Tragedy* he ended the work on a note of deep regret that the British elections of 1945 had interrupted his plans for the Potsdam meeting with Truman and Stalin: "All this negotiation was cut in twain and brought to an untimely conclusion by the results of the General Election." According to the memoirs he had planned a showdown with Stalin at Potsdam, when the fronts of the Allied armies faced each other, before the Americans made their "vast retirement . . . giving the heart and a great mass of Germany over to the Russians."

But the record does not bear out this heroic tale. He had already tried to persuade Truman that the American army should hold fast until a settlement had been reached with Stalin. At that time the American forces were into Czechoslovakia, near Prague, and a large part of eastern Germany. But Truman had no stomach for this kind of power politics, and he still had a war to fight in the Pacific. Churchill's plan for a showdown was never agreed, and it is doubtful he would have pressed it, even if he had won the elections. But it was to this vision that Churchill's thoughts must have been returning as he came back to the office that he had held in 1945.

The contrast between Churchill and his American colleagues could not have been greater. In Washington they were naturally preoccupied with the Korean War and with the great onslaught of worldwide communism that was being discovered in every policy document spewed out of the State Department and the White House. Washington also had a bad case of near-hysteria: the West was weak while Russia and China were strong; it would be years before the West would be strong enough to go to the bargaining table. Meanwhile, building a position of strength was the watchword. Even the skeptics among the Kremlinologists, Kennan and Bohlen, were not eager for negotiations; although they suspected that the Soviets were not as strong as claimed, they too preferred to await a better time for negotiations.

Churchill yielded to no one in his anticommunism. When some of the American leaders were in short pants, Churchill had urged the strangling of Bolshevism in its cradle. "Bolshevism is not a policy; it is a disease," he once said in the House of Commons (in 1920). Lenin's method, he wrote, was to save the world by blowing it up. Driven from office after the failure of the British campaign at Gallipoli in 1915, a campaign incidentally designed to rescue the Russian front, he became in 1919 the staunchest defender of British intervention in the Russian civil war. Later, in the 1920s, he attacked the Labour party as the handmaiden of the communists, and he did so to such good effect that he became chancellor of the exchequer in the Baldwin government from 1925 through 1929. Commenting on this campaign, he wrote that the Russian issue is "the one." And he even told Italian journalists that he would have been with "them" (the fascists) in the "triumphant struggle against the bestial appetites and passions of Leninism." Italy was the necessary "antidote to the Russian poison."

But his basic attitude was colored as much by history as by ideology. Russia remained a counterweight to Germany. In the 1930s the "dark menace of Soviet Russia" began to fade, and in its place reemerged the one power in the East that could thwart Hitler. Ideology had to recede and history to return. It had been Britain and Russia that had blocked Napoleon. Never mind the Crimea, or the menace at the Khyber Pass, or the echoes of Kipling; that was past. Confronted by Adolf Hitler, Britain had no choice but to recreate the coalition of 1914. The tragedy for Churchill was that his colleagues in the Tory leadership had learned the lesson of anticommunism only too well. Now they—the Cliveden set of appeasers—wanted to turn Hitler toward the east. When one member of this group, Lady Nancy Astor, visited Stalin, the Soviet leader asked after Churchill; appalled, her ladyship spat back, "He's finished." What is interesting is not Mrs. Astor's acid tongue, but Stalin's interest in a politician who was indeed widely regarded as "finished." Stalin's instincts, it turned out, were better than those of the titled lady from Brooklyn.

And before too long, Churchill and Stalin were comrades-in-arms. It was the German attack against Russia that prompted one of Churchill's most famous lines: if Hitler invaded hell, he, Churchill, would find an occasion to make a favorable remark in the House of Commons about the devil. And, of course, during the war Churchill steadfastly devoted himself to the final prize—the defeat of Hitler. For that Stalin was indispensable. Churchill worried that Stalin would conclude a separate peace early in the war, and on several occasions he chose not to challenge Stalin's postwar ambitions.

It was these territorial demands that Churchill found easiest to cope with, for they fitted his concept of international politics and history. Russia had a legitimate right to seek guarantees against Germany, which could be satisfied by a buffer in Eastern Europe; hence Churchill's spheres-of-influence bargain in 1944, conceding percentages of influence to Stalin. But there were also limits. Churchill was always dangling the Turkish Straits in front of Stalin, even conceding the Soviet Union a role as a naval power in the Mediterranean, a fairly safe concession, since Stalin had no navy. When Stalin, however, put in for a share of the German and Italian navies, Churchill was alarmed and found an excuse to avoid the subject. In their last encounter, at a dinner at Potsdam, Churchill poured Stalin a large glass of brandy to toast (Stalin usually drank from a small vodka glass); Stalin recognized the challenge and drank it down with a stroke and, glancing approvingly at Churchill, asked for a base in the Dardanelles.

These were memories stirring Churchill as he campaigned for office and won, and it was in this spirit of *Realpolitik* that he longed to return in the autumn of 1951. Earlier, during the failed election campaign of 1950, he had proposed a Great Power summit, only to be attacked for suggesting a "stunt." But again in his successful campaign a year later, he had proposed negotiations, and this time he had been attacked as a warmonger—a charge that stung him deeply, so much so that he sued the press, and won an out-of-court settlement. Even the mere suggestion of negotiations worried Washington, and with the approach of the British elections, Acheson and his cohorts were preparing papers to refute Churchill's anticipated proposal for a new Great Power meeting at the highest level. Churchill only sought a "narrow" lessening of tensions, they charged. There was one proposal that the American ambassador should approach Churchill with a warning during the campaign (a proposal fortunately not adopted).

After Churchill's election, Chip Bohlen wrote his appraisal of British policy and the differences with the United States as they stood in December 1951. Bohlen argued that the United States and the British had different concepts of how to deal with the Soviet Union.

The British were not reluctant to contemplate a settlement with the Soviet Union along the lines of "spheres of influence," which had a "special attraction" for Churchill. "There has not been in the British attitude and certainly not in Mr. Churchill any moral recoil from this method of settling big power differences." Bohlen concluded this analysis with the customary disclaimer on behalf of the United States:

"The British generally take the line that it is not only possible but desirable to make arrangements with the Soviet bloc as it stands, including Communist China, and that some reasonable durable basis for such a settlement could be found, whereas we don't believe that this is an acceptable assumption both for moral reasons and for practical reasons emanating from the nature of the Soviet state."

This was the self-righteous attitude that Churchill would confront in the years to come, but in a much more rigid distillation from the person he called "that Methodist preacher," John Foster Dulles.

These fearful men in Washington had overlooked something quite basic which, had they been at higher levels during the war, they would have understood instinctively. Churchill treasured above all else the special relationship with America. This was the alpha and omega of his foreign policy. To be sure, he was often exasperated and frustrated with the

Americans. He denounced them (privately), cursed Roosevelt's lack of experience, envied Truman's atomic power, and disdained Dulles's rigid diplomacy. During the war he had to endure Roosevelt's and Truman's baiting of the British lion's dying empire; he had to ward off Stalin's crude exploitation of the differences among the Anglo-Saxons. But Churchill understood power, and after the war power had flowed across the Atlantic from London to Washington.

The task of British diplomacy was to wed British interests to that awesome power. To do so meant guarding the special relationship from the attack of secondary issues—China, for example. The British had recognized the communist regime, and that divided them from the United States. The British were fearful that MacArthur, or Washington, would order a massive attack on China, allowing Stalin to swallow Europe. But Churchill warned Eden, before a particularly sensitive UN debate, not to lose the special relationship over Red China. On the other hand, he proposed to Truman that the British would follow the American lead in the Far East and the Americans would follow the British lead in the Middle East—a proposition that made Acheson apoplectic.

After his election, Churchill chose not to press the case for East-West negotiations until he had consolidated the special relationship. Unfortunately, Truman announced in late March 1952 that he would not stand for reelection. Moreover, the priority had to be given to finishing the reestablishment of German sovereignty and the pursuit of the European Defense Community. Churchill was wont to argue privately that it would be better to settle while Stalin was alive to guarantee any agreement would be implemented, but he decided to await the new American government, which it turned out would be led by his old wartime comrade Dwight D. Eisenhower. He told his confidants in June 1952 that if Eisenhower was elected, then Churchill would have another shot at a big-three meeting. He reasoned that it would be safer while Stalin lived than during a succession scramble. One idea of the prime minister's was to reopen the Potsdam Conference by means of a congress in Vienna; if, however, the Russians proved uncooperative, then the cold war would intensify.

Churchill contrived to visit Canada, and to stop in New York to see Eisenhower in December 1952 before the inauguration. He sounded Eisenhower out on the possibility of a new high-level meeting with Stalin. Eisenhower, not yet under Dulles's influence, was amenable, but he was more concerned about Korea. It was Stalin's death on March 5, 1953, that triggered both Churchill and Eisenhower into action. Churchill sent a telegram to Washington reminding Eisenhower of their conversation in New York and proposing a meeting with the new Soviet leaders. Eisenhower answered that Churchill's idea, among others, was being debated in Washington.

And indeed a debate had broken out in Washington between two views. The first school, mainly among Eisenhower's White House advisers, favored an early American initiative and a proposal to meet with Stalin's successors. The second group, mainly in the State Department, argued that such a meeting would be premature without careful preparations, and even dangerous in light of the growing problem over the ratification of the EDC in France.

The experts were of little help, and the new president complained that he had been warned about the possible death of Stalin for some time, but no one was prepared with any ideas. Hence, he had his advisers prepare some options, including that he deliver a foreign policy address. The CIA prepared a special intelligence appraisal of the Soviet scene that Allen Dulles presented to an NSC meeting, but it was too carefully hedged and virtually worthless. In the State Department, Chip Bohlen, who was preparing to depart for Moscow as the new ambassador, wrote a memorandum that predicted no essential change in policy, domestic or foreign. No one at that critical moment had the slightest clue to the inner workings of the Soviet leadership or of the immense trauma Stalin's successors were suffering. Nikita Khrushchev, the man who would come to dominate the situation, was scarcely mentioned in the various analyses that concentrated on Molotov, Malenkov, and Beria.

The view of the Kremlin that Stalin's death revealed among the highest levels of the American government was appalling. President Eisenhower said at an NSC meeting that he had believed that at the end of the war Stalin had wanted an easing of tensions, but the "Politburo had insisted on heightening the tempo of the cold war and Stalin had been obliged to make concession to this view." And he repeated this ludicrous interpretation a week later. Vice President Nixon speculated that Soviet policy would become harder, and Dulles eagerly agreed.

It must have been agony for Dulles to have to debate a proposal for a meeting with the Soviet leaders. He had prepared for years to take up the battle with the Soviet empire to proclaim the era of liberation, but he found himself in bureaucratic disputes about what should be included in a conciliatory presidential speech. Nevertheless, he carried the day on the policy; he argued strenuously against a proposal for a new meeting on Germany, which he said would bring down the French and Italian governments and make Anthony Eden's position untenable. This too was nonsense; the French wanted a four-power meeting. Eden supported a meeting, largely at Churchill's insistence. And Adenauer had begun to waiver, because he faced elections and thought he might disarm his domestic opponents by exposing Soviet hypocrisy on the German question.

Yet Dulles had a point: namely, that the real issue was not tactics but basic western strategy: either to move toward the final integration of West Germany in the alliance, or to open the door to a German settlement with the Soviet Union. Dulles, and to a slightly lesser extent Eisenhower, wanted to finish the project begun when Eisenhower was NATO commander: creating a European army to bring German power to bear on the East-West balance. It took no insight into the Kremlin's dark mysteries to guess that the Soviet Union would seek to delay German rearmament, and it was becoming clearer by the month that the target was France, the weakest but the most critical link in the alliance. If the French rejected the European army, then the Germans would have to either rearm with national forces or move toward a demilitarized and potentially neutral state, perhaps in some confederation with East Germany.

The western powers had succeeded in deflecting an appealing offer from Moscow in Stalin's last year (the peace note of March 10, 1952); but with his death all bets suddenly seemed to be off. This is what Dulles rightly feared.

But Churchill was not as fearful, because, first of all, he had never believed in the European army; if it expired, then a German national army would do just as well. As for the Soviets, they might delay and harass, but Churchill had in mind exploring a larger settlement in which the West would provide security guarantees to the USSR, while Moscow disengaged from Eastern Europe. This last scheme was a revival of the central idea that had animated the Locarno treaties of 1925. Then the idea was to break the stalemate between Germany and France and shore up the settlement in the West that followed World War I: Germany would accept its western border, giving up pretensions to Alsace-Lorraine; France would be reassured against Germany by a guarantee from the other powers, Britain and Italy. What Churchill thought in 1953 was that there might be an eastern Locarno, reassuring the Soviet Union against Germany.

The upshot was that in April–May 1953 both Eisenhower and Churchill delivered major speeches on East–West relations. Eisenhower spoke first in April and called for deeds, not words, including a Korean armistice and an Austrian peace treaty. Churchill read the draft in advance and mildly warned against a "frost nipping spring in the bud." Eisenhower reassured him that his speech would not freeze the buds of "sprouting decency, if indeed they are really coming about." The president, however, stopped well short of proposing new East–West negotiations. Churchill praised the speech but asked what the next step would be, and answered his own question by proposing a meeting of the three victorious powers: the United States, Britain, and the USSR. He even prepared a draft note to Molotov (Eden had been taken ill and was out of action because of two serious operations, and Churchill was his own foreign secretary). Dulles and Eisenhower vetoed the note to Molotov, which had been intended to pave the way for a summit, and warned him against rushing things. Nevertheless, in public Churchill pursued the same line in a major policy speech to the House of Commons on May 11, calling for a summit conference and explaining his idea for giving security assurances to Moscow through an eastern Locarno. The Churchillian challenge had been issued: to both Washington and Moscow.

The first result of Churchill's initiative was an agreement to hold a conference of the three western powers in Bermuda. The first round at least was Churchill's. And his excitement grew as the news from the East flowed in: riots in Berlin; shakeups in the Kremlin; the Doctor's Plot repudiated; Beria arrested. It was time that he and Eisenhower went to meet Malenkov, he insisted. But it was not to be. Fate intervened, in the form of a stroke on June 23 that left the old warrior partly paralyzed. For a few days it was thought he would die. With Eden desperately ill, the British government in effect was passed over to Lord Salisbury. The Bermuda conference was canceled, and the next steps in East-West diplomacy were given over to the foreign ministers, with Salisbury representing Britain.

At that meeting of foreign ministers in Washington, Churchill's presence was felt: to placate the French, who were still debating the EDC, a meeting would be proposed to the Soviets, but it was not the grand gesture, an act of visionary statesmanship but, rather, a bureaucratic move on the chessboard that it was hoped would be rebuffed. And Moscow was accommodating; it countered with a proposal for a five-power conference, including the Chinese, to discuss Asian matters. Nothing could have been more calculated to convince Dulles that the whole affair was a farce.

Churchill, as he recovered almost miraculously, sought to put diplomacy back on his original track: a new meeting of the western powers in Bermuda, and then on to the summit. He had been impressed by the moderate Soviet reaction to the Berlin riots. He speculated on meeting Malenkov "halfway," persuading the Russians to work for the good of Europe. He feared an opportunity would be lost, and inquired of his doctors whether he would be fit for a summit in September. But he began to encounter resistance, from his own advisers and from Dulles. He became bitter that the Democrats had not won; Eisenhower was both "weak and stupid," he exclaimed to his doctor, Lord Moran.

Gradually Churchill recovered his strength and began to marshal his arguments for a summit, arguments which he would have the opportunity to present at the rescheduled meeting with the Americans and the French at Bermuda.

One of the questions about a new summit meeting was what would be negotiated, or resolved. The American side wanted an armistice in Korea, but as a precondition to a meeting; the French wanted a settlement in Indochina, but again preferred to achieve it separately. All the powers wanted to conclude an Austrian treaty that would require a Soviet withdrawal. Again the Americans thought of it as a concession by Moscow, as the entrance price for further meetings, especially a summit. All were wary of negotiating on Germany, and both the western powers and the Soviets had adopted positions on Germany that were not likely to lead to compromise.

Churchill did not propose to answer the broad question of what would be settled. He argued that the time was ripe for a process to begin. Sometimes he talked of reopening Potsdam, sometimes he referred to an Austrian treaty as an act of "good faith" by the Soviets. Mostly, however, he dwelled on "meeting Malenkov." He marveled that the USSR was led by a man who had never met the western leaders or traveled abroad. He was persuaded that in a face-to-face encounter the western leaders could learn much. Depending on his mood, as well as the political temperature in Washington, he vacillated between a solo performance by himself and a three-power meeting that would include Eisenhower. More rarely, he spoke of a four-power summit that would include the French.

The main question Churchill kept posing was whether there was a "new look" in Moscow. In providing his own answer he made a set of broad points. First, the free world was rearming and confronting Soviet ambitions. This must have been an unpleasant shock, since after the war the Soviet leaders had thought they could push forward with impunity; now they had to conclude that their further efforts would confront a "struggle," and for this reason there might be a new look. Second was the Soviet economic situation. The combination of the two factors suggested that there was, in fact, a new look.

But what was to be done? Churchill argued that there had to be western reassurances for Moscow against another Hitler-like adventure. The Russians had a "right" to that reassurance. Second, the West could not recognize Soviet domination over their satellite states in East Europe, but the West did not propose to undo the situation by war.

In short, what Sir Winston proposed was a "reconnaissance in force," as he later explained it to Eisenhower. Had any other statesmen proposed such a vague undertaking he would have been quickly repudiated. The standard diplomatic approach to the summit was "careful preparation," but Churchill's reputation guaranteed him a hearing, and in the British press, at least, his position gained support.

Moreover, events began to break in a favorable direction for his position. Molotov, now restored to the foreign ministry, finally agreed to a four-power conference in Berlin, on the subjects of Germany and Austria. It was at the level of foreign ministers, however. The American side also began to soften somewhat, as Eisenhower gained confidence that he could handle East-West diplomacy.

A period of negotiations was opening in any case, both on European questions and on the Far East (a second foreign ministers' conference on Asia was to be held in Geneva, following the first meeting in Berlin). When the meeting in Berlin actually took place in January 1954, however, it was disappointing. Molotov took a hard line, insisting on a neutral Germany, and he brought in a new idea, a European security conference to conclude a nonaggression treaty and end the NATO alliance. After the conference Dulles claimed that there was a ripple of laughter when Molotov read his European security proposal (twenty years later a conference under that rubric did in fact open in Helsinki). Humorous or not, the intent was clear—to tempt Germany with neutrality as the price for reunification.

The Soviets did not take the Berlin meeting seriously, because they were shifting to another tack to defeat German rearmament—namely, killing the European Defense Community. The means were at hand, in a faraway place called Dien Bien Phu. The strategy was crude but effective: the Soviet Union would use its influence with Ho Chi Minh to permit the French to save face and withdraw gracefully from Indochina, but the price would be paid in Europe, the French defeat of the EDC. This was the situation that confronted the new French premier, Pierre Mendès-France.

The French leader quickly put himself in an impossible position by imposing his own deadline of July 20, 1954, to achieve a settlement in Indochina; the agreement ending the war and partitioning Vietnam was in fact signed on July 21, 1954. One month later, on August 23, the French National Assembly voted to shelve the European Defense Community treaty, in effect killing it. As this decisive showdown was taking shape, Churchill made one last effort to promote a high-level meeting. Without consulting his own cabinet, on his return from another meeting with Eisenhower he sent a private message to Molotov proposing a meeting with Malenkov.

Eisenhower was mildly critical of this initiative but seemed more interested in it than previously. Churchill's own cabinet was less enthusiastic, and there was a threat that Lord Salisbury might resign, on the ground that the cabinet needed to be consulted before such a major initiative. Eden also objected, but on substantive rather than constitutional grounds. Eden argued that the Russians might well propose an Austrian treaty to stop Germany's rearmament. Harold Macmillan, who was then minister for housing, was also opposed. Churchill retreated, using the appearance of a new Soviet diplomatic note proposing a high-level European security conference as the excuse not to press his own effort for a bilateral meeting.

The Soviets had outsmarted themselves. Churchill might have had the prestige to negotiate a new security order in Europe. The new Soviet leaders, however, inexperienced in foreign affairs, deferred to Molotov, whose strong suit was not negotiating but wrecking. He had learned to stall, to reject, to harass, to polemicize; no position was too ludicrous for Molotov (once he proposed that the USSR join NATO). His main strength was tenacity. He could and did stick to the same position for years; he had proved immune to blandishments when Hitler had offered to divide the world in 1940. And he was not about to give up his effort to block the rearmament of Germany. But the idea of a conciliatory diplomacy was his last refuge.

This rigidity, however, soon led to a stunning defeat. At first, Molotov had achieved a victory in the late summer of 1954. France was out of Indochina and German rearmament was dead. After four years, western plans were in a shambles. In the wake of the EDC defeat, there was a growing fear in Europe that Dulles would fulfill his threat to undertake an "agonizing reappraisal" of the American position as he had threatened in December. There was a fear that Germany, once again reduced to second-class status, would look to the East.

The western crisis galvanized Anthony Eden. In a whirlwind of nego-tiating, cajoling, and bargaining, he put together a new package that brought Germany into NATO as a full member, but restricted its arma-ment through the device of reviving the old, moribund Western European Union treaty. What made this work, however, was a historic British decision—to reverse four hundred years of history and commit Great Britain to maintaining a contingent of its army on the continent in defense of Western Europe.

Thus Winston Churchill's intuition that it might be time to reopen the Potsdam settlement came to be translated into a further, decisive step toward the division of Germany, and thereby the division of Europe.

6

EISENHOWER AT GENEVA

There were two final scenes to be played before the curtain could be drawn on Stalin's cold war. The first was the signature of the Austrian state treaty in May 1955. The second was the first postwar summit in Geneva, two months later, in July. Neither event changed what had already been decided by the end of 1954. But the symbolism was nevertheless important.

The Austrian state treaty was Molotov's last card in the struggle over Germany. Khrushchev later claimed that Molotov balked at playing this trump, which he had been hoarding for ten years. If true, it would not be surprising. For Austria was a microcosm of Soviet foreign policy. It had little strategic value, unless it was under total Soviet control. Early in the postwar period, the Soviets decided not to try to convert their half of Austria to a communist puppet. Moreover, Austria had a central government from the start, and in contrast to Germany the Soviets maintained a semblance of four-power control in Vienna. At any point an Austrian peace treaty could have been signed. But the Soviets linked it to the German question on the calculation that at some point it might be an inducement to a German settlement. This turned out to be a miscalculation, because Rhineland Germany, under the guidance of Konrad Adenauer, could not have cared less what happened to Austria—which had earned the unenviable reputation of one of Hitler's most loyal satrapies.

For years the Austrian question was dormant. After Stalin died, however, Eisenhower had made an Austrian treaty one of the "deeds" that the new leaders in Moscow would have to perform to satisfy western conditions for a new summit. By late 1954, however, the Austrian issue had become a potential nightmare; it was greatly feared that Soviet concessions in Austria would derail the train of West Germany's alliance with Western Europe as provided by the Paris agreements engineered by Eden.

The Soviet Union did play the Austrian card. But the Austrian treaty remains something of a puzzle. As feared, the Soviets made concessions on the neutral status of Austria that were designed to affect the German question. The major tactic was to separate the German and Austrian issues and offer to sign an Austrian treaty immediately. With Germany in mind the Soviets also offered to permit Austria to have a small national army, if it would proclaim its neutrality, which was then to be guaranteed by the former occupying powers. This was the formula that Dulles and his colleagues feared would take hold in Germany.

Until 1955, American policy had been to "vigorously resist the neutralization of Austria as contrary to U.S. interests," a policy enshrined in various NSC directives. Dulles made some attempt to brush off the Soviet initiative. But it was too inviting for the Austrians, who feared that with the growing division of Europe, Austria might miss its last chance for a Soviet withdrawal. Yet Molotov did not move until very late in the game, surfacing his scheme for neutralization during a visit to Moscow by the Austrian leaders in April 1955. By then it was much too late to have a real impact on Germany, and by then the new dialogue over a summit meeting was also beginning. Molotov was no fool and no neophyte. He must have recognized that the timing of his maneuver was all wrong.

Thus, there may well be a different explanation for Soviet policy. Rather than being a desperate, last-minute effort to stave off German rearmament in NATO, it may have been a defensive Soviet reaction, a decision to create a buffer between Germany and Eastern Europe, and to prevent the Allies from incorporating a rump Austria into the western alliance.

Until the very last moment, Dulles suspected trickery—"characteristic trickery" was his phrase. He was worried that neutrality would spread and affect the "little" countries. Finally it dawned on him that the Austrian treaty was a victory—the result of steadfast western determination. As the chancellor of Austria, Julius Raab, pointed out to Dulles, the Russians were withdrawing eastward, militarily and economically. Dulles eventually concluded that the Austrian treaty, signed on May 10, 1955, was the "first fruit" of a united NATO. It was also the ticket to the four-power summit meeting that Dulles had resisted since Stalin's death.

It would be comforting if the first postwar summit had been the product of a clever design, either in the East or West, or both. But it came about as a stumbling, bumbling affair, a mixture of politics and statesmanship. The godfather, of course, was Winston Churchill, but by the time of the summit in July 1955 he was in retirement. His successor, Anthony Eden, had originally resisted a summit and preferred a foreign ministers' meeting. Having finally succeeded in forcing Churchill to retire, Eden switched his position and began to urge a summit. The British were now committed to the continent by the Paris agreements, and this changed London's perspective. Now it was time for diplomacy. Moreover, Eden would soon have to face a general election. In early May, Eden urged Eisenhower to attend a "top-level" meeting, sounding much like Churchill in his arguments. Eisenhower replied that he was a "bit surprised" at Eden's new proposals, but it became clear that after the Austrian treaty, the leaders of the four powers would have to meet.

Then Dulles also began to come around, but fearing what would happen at a summit of the top leaders, as all foreign ministers fear when their chiefs assemble, he proposed to Eisenhower a general meeting to determine whether "ways and means could be found to settle differences." In that case, Dulles argued, "the harm is held to a minimum." Eisenhower was still reluctant to "rush into" a summit, and was disturbed by French and British eagerness. But he was warming to the idea. At first he thought that the summit might be ceremonial, a sort of ribbon-cutting opening, after which the foreign ministers would take over. Eisenhower even toyed with the notion that Nixon could lead the U.S. summit delegation.

In a memorandum to the British cabinet, Eden argued that the time was ripe, because with nuclear saturation the western position would inevitably get weaker; the signing of the Paris agreement incorporating Germany into NATO would be a high point. Unlike Dulles, who had a vague scheme for a general meeting, Eden advocated a "definite, if limited" result.

The real moving force was France. First it was Pierre Mendès-France, having presided over the defeat of the EDC, who now insisted that he could not guarantee the ratification of the Paris agreements by the Parliament without a four-power summit. When he met resistance from Dulles, he blithely proposed that France and Russia meet—sending shudders through the German government, which then appealed to Dulles. In February 1955, Mendès-France was replaced by Edgar Faure as prime minister with Antoine Pinay at the Quai d'Orsay. However, they took almost the same position. As Molotov's Austrian gambit developed, Adenauer became increasingly alarmed. He finally conceded that there might have to be a summit, but was adamantly opposed to any serious negotiations. Later, for domestic political reasons, he supported western proposals on German unification to be presented to Moscow.

With the signature of the Austrian treaty in May, U.S. resistance melted and Eisenhower agreed to a summit for July. At the end of a cabinet meeting, Eisenhower smiled and said he was getting the reputation of a very peaceful man, surrounded by warmongers. Dulles commented that such a situation was not without its advantages. And then Dulles proceeded to warn the assembled cabinet that the real dangers of the summit were projects that the Soviets could use to confirm American acceptance of the East European satellites and of international communism. On those two fronts the United States would have to launch a counteroffensive.

After all of this debate about a summit, Washington found itself ill-prepared, intellectually and practically. At first Eisenhower thought that the meeting would simply consider "general attitudes" on the solutions of outstanding problems. Later, he became more concerned that the western participants should have something to say. Dulles found it more and more difficult to explain Soviet policy, which confounded his simple-minded quotations from Stalin's early writings *(Problems of Leninism)*. Nevertheless, he decided that nothing fundamental had changed, despite Stalin's death. And in this he found support in the academic community and his brother's CIA intelligence estimates. The best explanation, the Dulles brothers decided, was that the Soviets suffered from a leadership crisis, faced major economic problems, and therefore needed a "pause," and some reductions in the burden of armaments (themes that were to become all too familiar). Consequently, the West would have to remain "resolute." Eisenhower's instincts warned him that there might be more involved than this simplified explanation, but he was unsure of himself.

Konrad Adenauer suffered no uncertainties. He had been invited to Moscow by the new leaders and planned to visit in September after the summit. But he needed something he could hold on to—a proposal for German unity, which was sure to be rejected by Moscow but which he could parade before the German electorate. So he appealed for something at the summit. Eden was somewhat sympathetic, also in part for his own domestic political reasons. But once the British foreign office began to turn over the issues, it conceived of a new approach: thinning out military forces in various zones built around a divided Germany. Even Adenauer had a private scheme for such thinned-out areas. All of this frightened Dulles, who preferred to stand pat. But Dulles had to admit that the West's hand was a strong one. Yet he anticipated that the western position would weaken over time.

The western powers were unprepared. At the very last minute, Dulles asked Eisenhower's former special assistant for security affairs C. D. Jackson to meet with him in Washington and unburdened himself to Jackson after a private dinner. Dulles greatly feared that Eisenhower would collapse at the summit because of his good nature, and that he, Dulles, would have to throw himself into the fray to save the Republic. Jackson was appalled at this, and he tried to cheer up his morbid secretary. One could well imagine Eisenhower's reaction had he been informed of this pathetic last-minute display.

Dulles's moment of near-hysteria was not unique. For on the eastern side as well there was near-panic among the new leaders who would attend, Nikolai Bulganin and Nikita Khrushchev. Neither had any experience in international diplomacy. Both feared that they would be in a weak position. Khrushchev, reacting to American press speculation about the Kremlin's weakness, harangued the American deputy ambassador at a July 4 reception in Moscow that was widely reported as a friendly gesture. In reality, Khrushchev was mildly threatening, warning that they were not coming to Geneva on "broken legs." Khrushchev was mortified that the Soviet aircraft that flew to Geneva was smaller than the American plane. When he flew to Washington four years later he came in a new jet that nearly exhausted its fuel by flying nonstop.

The speculation that the Soviet leaders would use the summit to thwart German association with NATO proved wrong. The reason was simple: by mid-1955 the Soviets had accepted the division of Germany and, consequently, German rearmament. In turn, they intended to elevate East Germany to a sovereign state. By receiving Adenauer in Moscow, the formal division of Germany would be sealed, at least cosmetically. Thus the window of opportunity for German unity, if it ever really existed, was closing fast. In Moscow, Ambassador Bohlen caught this nuance, and so did the CIA in its final pre-summit intelligence estimate. Both agreed that the Soviets were reconciling themselves to the division of Germany—not forever, but for a significant period. Moscow could not block the reemergence of Germany, but it could limit the consequences of a rump state on the Rhine.

This meant that the problem of western military power would not be attacked through Germany, as a Trojan horse in NATO, but more indirectly by increasingly complicated and elaborate schemes for European security, the heart of which was the withdrawal of American nuclear weapons from Europe. Without realizing it, the western powers in countering with their own European security plans were to play into Soviet hands—though the Soviets also did not anticipate that within two years a great debate would break out over American "disengagement" from Europe.

As a historic event the Geneva summit (July 18–23, 1955) was surprisingly bland. Not much happened on the substance of the cold war. The Soviet side on July 20 presented an elaborate European security treaty featuring a nonaggression plan. The western side (Eden) countered with a plea for German unity. Eisenhower surprised everyone with his proposal for "open skies" (the lights went out in the conference room as he finished explaining his proposal, causing a moment of humor). The press was intrigued by the private meeting between the two old soldiers, Eisenhower and Marshal Zhukov, who had been rehabilitated after Stalin's death. Nothing came of these meetings, but in general the western side concluded that Khrushchev was in charge. The Soviet side passed a "confidential" message that their leaders were impressed with Eisenhower, who was "very forceful and a sincere man." In his memoirs, however, Khrushchev disparaged Eisenhower for paying too much attention to Dulles.

The Soviets (Molotov) made it clear that henceforth Germany would be folded into the broader topic of European security. Eisenhower recognized that this new linkage was a critical difference, because the western powers wanted priority to go to the German question. If there was an innovation, it was that "disarmament" was discussed for the first time at the summit. Khrushchev told Eisenhower that his open-skies proposal was propaganda, and Eisenhower challenged the Soviet leader to take him up on it. Khrushchev then "ran out," according to the president's account. Despite such friction, for Eisenhower the most obvious result was the "unshakable personal friendliness of the Russian delegation"—at least this is what he told congressmen afterward.

The result of this "historic summit," held ten years after Potsdam, was aptly summed up by Harold Macmillan, then the British foreign secretary: "There ain't gonna be no war," he was quoted as saying. And, put more elegantly, this was the broad conclusion of both the statesmen and the outside observers. Churchill had said that he wanted to discuss the "supreme issues," and in effect this is what had happened. The cold war in Europe and Asia would continue, but it would not lead to a shooting war between East and West. That seemed to be the broad conclusion of

Geneva. Eden put it this way in his memoirs: "Each country present learnt that no country attending wanted war and each understood why . . . the deterrent power of nuclear weapons." In his memoirs, Eisenhower was more guarded: "I believe the Geneva conference was a limited success. The record was established: all could now see the nature of Soviet diplomatic tactics. . . ."

The division of Germany was confirmed. If there had been a fleeting moment of opportunity, opened by Stalin's peace note of March 1952, it was now closed definitively. But this was also somewhat deceptive. True, the division of Germany was implicitly accepted. But not explicitly, because the western powers were still haunted by the ghost of Yalta. Any hint of acceptance of the status quo had to be squashed. So after the summit the West emphasized its refusal to recognize the Soviet sphere.

Had Stalin lived, this might have been swallowed in Moscow as a tolerable bit of hypocrisy, as long as the West did not act on its pretensions. But this western recalcitrance against accepting the Soviet empire in Eastern Europe reckoned without the new leaders, especially Khrushchev. It rankled that the West maintained a self-righteous refusal to acknowledge what Stalin had won after the war. Confirming those wartime and postwar gains became an obsession with Khrushchev. Thus it was that Geneva sowed the seeds for the next phase in the cold war, which would lead finally to the confrontation in Cuba.

Without knowing it, another dimension of the new cold war was present at Geneva—the Soviet leap into the third world, beginning with Egypt. In one of their meetings at Geneva, Dulles casually told Eden and Macmillan that the United States had turned down a request from Nasser for weapons; Nasser had threatened to turn to the Soviets. Eden expressed his doubts that this would happen. Yet at that very moment, while the heads of government talked at Geneva, a Soviet ship was loading Czech arms for Egypt, and the first steps toward the Suez crisis had been taken.

There would be no world war—that was now clear; but there would also not be the grand settlement that Churchill had hoped for. After Geneva, Trotsky's old prescription for Soviet foreign policy after the

Brest-Litovsk treaty of 1918—neither war nor peace—would have been appropriate to describe the period about to begin.

As long as this Trotskyite formula was the prevailing policy in Moscow, the West could not go beyond peaceful coexistence in its relations with the Soviet Union. When this ambivalence about the clash between state interests and world revolution was challenged by Gorbachev, an end to the cold war finally became possible.

EISENHOWER AND KHRUSHCHEV

7

For the first decade of the cold war, nuclear weapons played a surprisingly secondary role. They did not figure at all in the first major crisis, the Berlin blockade. They were a factor in the debate about how to fight the Korean War, but there was no serious plan to use them. Stalin deprecated the weapons, even after the Soviet Union exploded an atomic device in 1949. On his orders, his military theorists dutifully brushed aside any idea that these new weapons could determine the outcome of the war. American military strategists were not that foolish, but by and large the World War II generation saw atomic bombs as another category of weaponry—highly destructive, to be sure, but not extraordinarily so if measured against all of the factors affecting the outcome of a war.

This attitude began to change in the mid-1950s, for some obvious reasons. First there was the creation of the hydrogen bomb, with huge increases in power. Second was the appearance of longer-range rockets and missiles, which raised the possibility of delivering nuclear warheads across continents. And finally, there was the attitude of Nikita Khrushchev, who by no means shared Stalin's contempt for these new weapons. Indeed, Khrushchev saw the chance to put the United States under a direct and severe threat. He had no clear concept of what a nuclear strategy might be, but he keenly sensed that for the first time the Soviet Union could leapfrog the defensive barriers that the West had constructed around the USSR. This startling simple conclusion would take the cold war deeper and deeper into uncharted and dangerous waters.

Eisenhower belonged to the school that thought of nuclear weapons as another form of offensive power, but not truly unique—at least before 1955 and before the major advances in missile technology. He could contemplate the use of atomic weapons. The Eisenhower administration adopted in October 1953 a basic national security policy (NSC 161/2) stating that atomic weapons should be considered as "available" as other weapons. This was roughly the same view as that of the Truman administration. Eisenhower indirectly threatened to use atomic weapons in Korea shortly after taking office, a threat which he believed produced serious negotiations to end the war. He casually told Churchill in January 1954 that if the Chinese communists launched an offensive in Korea he would use nuclear weapons; Churchill and Eden were stunned and argued vehemently against it.

Korea was in a special category, however, because the United States was at war. In other situations Eisenhower's views were more prudent. In 1954, during the siege of Dien Bien Phu, Eisenhower entertained a plan for an American atomic strike to save the encircled French, advocated by Dulles and the Joint Chiefs of Staff. But in the end he turned against the idea because it seemed technically infeasible to attack the Vietminh forces without wiping out the French and Dien Bien Phu. And, more important, he was reluctant to wage war in Asia. Again, in 1955 during the Taiwan Straits crisis, he considered an atomic strike on the mainland. The Chinese communists had begun a campaign of shelling the offshore islands, held by Chinese nationalist forces, which Eisenhower believed had to be defended, lest Formosa (Taiwan) itself be attacked. When faced with an American atomic threat, albeit an ambiguous one, the Chinese backed away from a confrontation. Eisenhower later claimed that he would have ordered atomic strikes "only" on military targets on the mainland.

On these occasions it was not the horror of atomic weapons that was decisive in restraining Eisenhower, but the consequences of using military force. Eisenhower understood, as military men do, that a small use of force was as dangerous as a massive use. The Korean War, he once said, could not be won by small battles for small hills. Thus in Indochina and the Taiwan Straits he was more persuaded by the geopolitics of the crisis than by the feasibility of the weapons to be employed. Eisenhower profoundly believed that a war in Asia would become a war against Russia, or at least should be, because the Soviet Union was the main enemy (almost the same position taken by Dean Acheson). The official intelligence estimate during the Taiwan crisis was that the USSR would have to come into a war to save China. In such a war, Eisenhower told his aides, everything had to be subordinate to winning a victory. The dilemma was that the United States could not start such a war but had to wait to be struck. As the official predictions of casualties grew in the event of a nuclear attack, Eisenhower became more and more uneasy with a strategy and ethic that dictated waiting to be struck. He was frustrated by a strategy in which nuclear weapons seemed to play a peripheral offensive role. It was this frustration that made massive retaliation an attractive option.

Eisenhower was upset by the huge demands of the defense budgets ($35 billion in 1953) and was convinced that there was money to be saved; a conservative Midwesterner, he believed in trying to balance the budget. Eventually he approved the "new look" defense strategy that tried to achieve greater firepower for less cost (a "bigger bang for a buck"). Thus the idea of shifting gradually to a nuclear strategy and threatening to retaliate was appealing, but primarily as a means of deterrence. Dulles gloried in the brinkmanship, which irritated Eisenhower, who deplored the elements of bluff when it came to war and peace. The general strategy of deterrence appealed to the Eisenhower administration, but massive retaliation was more appropriate to containment than Dulles's other doctrine of "liberation" of Eastern Europe. Eisenhower linked the twin ideas of checking the communist advance and then rolling it back.

Both doctrines—massive retaliation and liberation—had a synthetic quality, reflecting Dulles's pedantic approach to foreign policy. Eisenhower recognized their limits. In one of their very early discussions, Eisenhower said to Dulles that he could not see how massive retaliation could be applied against the famous Soviet salami tactics, small moves against hostile positions. Nor was Eisenhower ever disposed to go to war for Eastern Europe—neither was Dulles, for that matter. The NSC planning papers included no serious program for liberating Eastern Europe. But the excessive rhetoric about liberation set up the conditions for two severe shocks and defeats: the Hungarian uprising and Khrushchev's Sputnik blackmail.

Ironically, both crises grew out of the struggle over colonialism and imperialism at Suez. After World War II, the British became increasingly worried about Egypt, especially after the colonels' revolt overthrew King Farouk. London tried to interest Washington in the Middle East, but even Churchill could not get much sympathy, let alone support. Eisenhower, following the pattern of Truman and Roosevelt, had little sympathy for the British empire, or for the French empire for that matter. Roosevelt teased Churchill shamelessly about his empire, and Truman was completely insensitive to British concerns. Eisenhower had a slightly better appreciation, recognizing that the collapse of the old colonial empires might create a battleground with the communists. Nevertheless, Eisenhower was scornful of the British and French for their efforts to preserve their rotting empires. While Stalin lived, the breakup of colonialism was not an urgent threat, because Stalin was contemptuous of these backward areas, often led by dangerously charismatic figures well beyond Soviet control. Khrushchev and his colleagues, however, saw opportunities where Stalin saw dangerous exposures. And consequently, when the opening was provided by Nasser in 1955, Moscow decided to move.

At first, even this radical break in Soviet policy did not make much difference to Washington. But Eden was increasingly obsessed by the threat not simply to the old colonial lifeline to India, which had been independent since 1947, but to the British position in Jordan and Iraq. And he constantly warned Eisenhower of the dangers of communist collaboration with the radical Arabs. He framed the test in terms of appeasement or support for allies in the Baghdad Pact. Later, when accused by his critics of falsely casting the issue in terms of Munich, Eden replied that he saw Nasser not as another Hitler but as another Mussolini. Thus for Eden the crisis was a rerun of Ethiopia—where twenty years earlier British vacillation had failed to deter Italy and encouraged Hitler.

As the crisis deepened, Dulles continued to search for some formula to turn over the control of the Suez Canal to Nasser. Gradually he began to share Eden's alarm. Some in the British establishment came to believe that Dulles would support their military effort to take over the canal and drive Nasser from power. But if so, they reckoned without Eisenhower. When confronted by the fact of the British-French invasion at Suez in October 1956, the president was outraged and frustrated—outraged that he had been deceived by his allies (who had refused to inform him in advance), and frustrated by the amateurish botch the British and French made of their military operations. In any case, he intervened against the British and French by denouncing their operation, reducing Eden to tears at one point and destroying his career. Churchill had been right: Eden did not have the stuff for leadership.

Nevertheless, the United States paid a high price for Eden's folly and faintheartedness. For the next fifteen years America was increasingly identified with the colonialist cause in the Middle East, and with Israel. The Soviet Union benefited enormously, and its penetration of the Middle East reached truly alarming proportions during the Vietnam War and after the Six-Day War in 1967. Thus the Middle East became a new arena for the struggle between East and West, much as Eden had forecast.

The ultimate irony was that in time the British would withdraw altogether from the area "East of Suez," leaving the United States to man the front line from the Khyber Pass to Marrakesh. Eisenhower launched this new American mission in early 1957, when in a speech he said that "Russia's rulers have long sought to dominate the Middle East. This was true of the czars and it is true of the Bolsheviks." His counter was the Eisenhower doctrine: any country threatened by "overt armed aggression" could rely on the United States.

But the crisis over Suez had a more immediate and dangerous consequence. As the crisis unfolded, at a safe moment, Khrushchev issued the first missile warning of the cold war, not against the United States but against the British and French. The language of the Soviet diplomatic note of November 5, 1956, signed by Bulganin, was elliptical and appropriately

94

vague, but the meaning was clear. For the first time Moscow had the reach to attack one of America's allies, and with the devastating power of the atom. True, the United States could strike back, but for the first time a new question was raised: would America retaliate if it meant a threat to the continental United States?

During the crisis, Eisenhower made it clear that he would retaliate. Well afterward he recalled that he had told the Russians it would be a "global war." Eden claimed that the Soviet threat "need not be taken literally," and took the opportunity to reply that the Soviets had been "ruthlessly crushing" the heroic resistance in Hungary. Nevertheless, a serious gap had been revealed in the concept of massive retaliation. As long as Khrushchev could not threaten the United States directly, the logic of deterrence was intact, but should the Soviet Union ever acquire a longer-range missile, then what?

In the fall of 1956, such thoughts were distant clouds. Khrushchev was gaining a reputation for bluff and tough talk; his rocket-rattling at Suez seemed no more than that. The British and French were unnerved, but Eisenhower quickly reestablished a working relationship with the new government of Harold Macmillan, his old wartime comrade. Of immediate concern was the revolt in Hungary which had broken out during the Suez confrontation. Soviet troops had intervened and brutally put down a brief uprising in Budapest. Then the Soviet leaders installed János Kádár as their new puppet and murdered the former premier, Imre Nagy, who had tried to follow Khrushchev's anti-Stalinism. Over thirty years later Kádár was caught up in another change in Soviet policy and was himself removed from power and expelled from the party hierarchy. Nagy was publicly rehabilitated—a sort of poetic justice.

The Soviet leaders had themselves to blame for the Hungarian revolution. Khrushchev, in unleashing his attack on Stalin, had called into question the legitimacy of all of East Europe's satraps governed by little Stalinists, especially the more odious ones such as Mátyás Rákosi in Budapest. Once the dam broke against the old guard in Budapest (and in Warsaw), the inevitable result was a crisis.

It was temporarily comforting in the West that the communist systems seemed totally discredited, but the stark fact was that the United States did nothing, after preaching liberation for four years. At a NATO meeting after the Hungarian crisis, Dulles virtually buried any thought of liberation; he said privately to his NATO colleagues that under present world conditions "we could not accept the concept of each nation, subject to injustice, attempting to remedy that injustice by force. That would let loose forces which would almost surely lead to World War III, particularly given the present predicament and power of Soviet rulers."

Thus the acceptance of division of Europe which had been implicit at the four-power summit in Geneva in 1955 was now confirmed explicitly. Europe was sharply divided into two spheres, almost exactly along the lines Stalin had indicated more than a decade earlier to Churchill.

This settling down in Europe might have worked, except for two facts of political psychology: the Americans' chagrin at being exposed as frauds and Khrushchev's pugnacious megalomania. Dulles and Eisenhower continued to preach liberation and proclaim their refusal to accept the status quo in Europe. This refusal to acknowledge reality was galling to Khrushchev, and he became obsessed with forcing the recognition of his dominance in the East. (And in 1958 he finally found the vehicle to force the issue—the exposed and vulnerable western position in Berlin.)

Despite Hungary and Suez, and Khrushchev's bluster, East-West relations maintained a surprisingly steady course during most of 1957. There were arms control and disarmament negotiations in Geneva that produced laborious formulas for complete disarmament; there was a scheme for inspection zones to guard against surprise attacks by bombers flying over the North Pole. And there were elaborate schemes for German confederations published in East Berlin.

There was also a confrontation among the Soviet leaders, in which Khrushchev emerged triumphant over a formidable combination of Malenkov, Molotov, and Kaganovich, and the recently appointed foreign minister, Dimitri Shepilov (whose purge brought Andrei Gromyko to the foreign ministry for the next twenty-eight years). In the recriminations and revelations that followed this "antiparty" crisis, Molotov was accused of having opposed several conciliatory policies, including the Austrian state treaty and the opening to Tito. Thus there were reasons to believe that Khrushchev's victory would lead to an easing of tensions, especially since in the Kremlin crisis, Marshal Zhukov, Eisenhower's old comrade, had played a key role in bringing the support of the armed forces behind Khrushchev.

In September 1957, Ambassador Thompson gave his interpretation to the State Department to the effect that Khrushchev "really wants and is almost forced to a détente in relations with the West." The ambassador was also "optimistic in the long range about Soviet seriousness in the disarmament situation." His reasoning was that Khrushchev needed to tend to his economic reforms, especially his decentralization plans and the new-lands program for agriculture, and resources would have to be diverted from the military. Khrushchev seemed to be a "new type" of Soviet leader, Thompson concluded. This optimism turned out to be ominously wrong. Khrushchev was a new type, though not in the sense western observers had hoped. He proved to be an irresponsible and dangerous gambler.

What gave him the opportunity and courage to undertake his adventurous thrusts was a simple technical feat. In October the Soviet Union announced that it had launched into near earth orbit an artificial earth satellite. Suddenly, Khrushchev's boasts that the Soviet Union had a long-range missile capability had to be taken with deadly seriousness. As this elementary fact began to sink in, there was a growing sense of panic in western capitals. The one thing that had seemed certain in the postwar world was American technological superiority—and now belief in that was shattered. The pervasive concern was heightened when the United States failed in its launch of a small space vehicle. Only President Eisenhower seemed to take events calmly. He understood better than most the extreme difficulties of moving from a small prototype missile launched by careful scientists to a true military weapons capability. He doubted the Soviets had reached that stage, but this was largely based on his instinct (reliable, as it turned out), and the facts seemed to be working against the president. There was a sensational report of a blue-ribbon committee (led by businessman Rowan Gaither) that predicted a massive missile gap. The United States seemed to be facing the "gravest danger in its history," one reporter wrote about the report.

Khrushchev lost no time in exploiting his opening. Since the Hungarian uprising, Soviet policy had been a holding operation. Now Khrushchev embarked on a long, bitter offensive designed to humiliate the West, under the pressure of the missile gap. The offensive would not end until Khrushchev himself was humiliated in Cuba.

His first step was to demand a new summit meeting. He dramatized the new atmosphere by ordering his representative to walk out of the UN disarmament talks. Then he explained that the purpose of a summit meeting would be to confirm the postwar status quo, i.e., to force the West to recognize Stalin's conquests in Europe. "Only one thing is needed," Khrushchev insisted, "to recognize what has historically taken place. . . . There must be no interference in their [Eastern Europe's] affairs." Later he explained more directly that "the status quo must be recognized, that is to say the fact that there are two systems of states in the world. . . ."

Nowhere was the impact of the Sputnik and Khrushchev's subsequent political offensive greater than in West Germany. For Konrad Adenauer had staked Germany's future on close alliance with the West on the simple theory that western strength would over time force the Soviet Union to disgorge Stalin's gains. Then, and only then, would Germany be reunited. He had campaigned successfully on this alliance with the West, and had won a strong mandate. Now his theory seemed in doubt.

And doubts were raised in the alliance, as well as in Germany. Khrushchev had caught the alliance in the process of deploying some short-range tactical nuclear weapons in Germany. Khrushchev, of course, campaigned against the deployment; but more sober voices in the West also raised questions. Among them was George Kennan's. Now out of office, in a series of widely publicized lectures he called for the denuclearization of Germany and the disengagement of both American and Soviet forces from Central Europe. Inside Germany the same general proposition was adopted by the opposition Social Democrats, who argued that the German question had to be addressed before it was too late. The Soviets played to this sentiment by warning that German acceptance of new rocket launchers from the Americans would mean the end to any chance for German unification. And then the Soviets, through the Poles, set forth the idea of an atomic free zone, covering the two Germanies, Poland, and Czechoslovakia (a plan named for Polish foreign minister Adam Rapacki).

In this debate the West German Socialists revived the old question of the "lost opportunity" of March 1952, when Stalin had sent his peace note to the West. The Socialists warned another opportunity would be lost if the Germans did not renounce American nuclear weapons and open a dialogue with the East. Adenauer argued that any zone of special armaments would freeze the division of Germany. The German debate revealed in startling clarity the clash between the two approaches that would echo down through the decades. The German Socialists argued that through a détente and arms limitations there would be a chance of persuading Moscow to unify the German nation. Adenauer argued the opposite: that only through a position of strength, based on close association with the West, could Germany hope for unity; any scheme that created doubts of German loyalty in the West had to be avoided, and any scheme that suggested Germany would be singled out as a special zone outside the alliance had to be fought like the plague. This broad debate would erupt at intervals for thirty years, and reappear in 1989 after East Germany collapsed. Then the West German chancellor, Helmut Kohl, adopted the old eastern position of unification through a loose confederation.

Adenauer, under domestic pressures, forced through the Bundestag a resolution accepting American atomic weapons, but then suggested that a four-power summit dealing with disarmament might be acceptable. Dulles resisted his old friend, however. He distrusted summits in principle, and at this moment he correctly argued that there could not be a new summit that disregarded the failure of the post-summit negotiations after

1955. In other words, the two issues of the Geneva summit—Germany and European security—had to be addressed.

Khrushchev was ready for this argument. He revealed that the Soviet priorities had indeed changed since his Geneva summit with Eisenhower: security issues would have to take priority, while the German question had to be restricted to signing a German peace treaty. The question of unification would be left for the two German states. The only basis for unification, Khrushchev claimed, was to recognize the historical fact that there were "two states with different social systems." Finally, Khrushchev suggested that the definition of Germany's future military status might influence the Soviet position on unity. It was a clever and insidious package, but it concealed a much harsher position. Khrushchev wanted to keep Germany divided, but to weaken the western part by undermining its position in the western alliance and restricting its armaments.

Nevertheless, Khrushchev was not well suited to the intricacies of political warfare by nuance and maneuver. He preferred the frontal assault, and by the summer of 1958 he had tired of diplomacy, even though the western powers were moving toward a summit meeting. He began to prepare a new surprise attack that would throw the crisis into a new phase. He would demand that the West get out of Berlin.

8/0

BERLIN

If there was a monument to the cold war, it was the Berlin Wall. Memories fade of Yalta and Potsdam, of Korea, even of Vietnam. But for almost thirty years the Wall was grim testimony to the longest and most dangerous crisis of the cold war. The crisis began in Berlin because Germany was central to the ambitions of both Stalin and Khrushchev. In 1948 and again a decade later, Berlin was the most immediate target, but the cold war was ultimately about the future of Germany, and when the Wall was opened, the cold war was over.

The second Berlin crisis unfolded in three phases. It began with the first Soviet ultimatum of the cold war: Khrushchev's demand (November 27, 1958) that the West give up its rights in Berlin and evacuate the city within six months. This phase lasted until May 1960, when the four-power summit in Paris collapsed over Khrushchev's insistence that Eisenhower apologize for the U-2 affair.

The next phase bridged the last months of the Eisenhower presidency and the beginning of Kennedy's. Again an ultimatum was delivered by Khrushchev, who demanded at the Vienna summit with Kennedy that a settlement be reached by the end of the year (1961). This particular phase, however, proved to be a brief one, because in August 1961 Khrushchev ordered the barbed wire and concrete blocks to be erected along the city's dividing line. The infamous Wall had begun. This was the second calamity for the West, following the failure of the Paris summit over the U-2 incident. The Wall should have eased if not ended the crisis by shutting down the disastrous flow of East German refugees.

But the confrontation continued into its third and final phase because the crisis was not only about Berlin and Germany but about the balance of power. Khrushchev had launched a global offensive—in the Middle East, in Laos, in the Congo—on the calculation that the "correlation of forces," as the communists were fond of calling it, had shifted irretrievably in the Soviet Union's favor. The symbol of this shift was the Sputnik. This claim of a new balance of power was the underlying theme of Khrushchev's Berlin ultimatum of November 1958. By the end of 1961, however, the feared missile gap had been exposed as a myth. For Khrushchev the harsh new fact was that the Soviets were falling behind in the strategic race. But the instrument for retrieving the balance was at hand, a missile base in Cuba.

This last and definitive phase of the four-year crisis had little to do with the defense of Cuba, as Khrushchev claimed and his latter-day apologists have echoed. The confrontation in Cuba was about global power. It was a classic case of Lenin's question: *kto-kvo*—who gets whom? Its resolution in October 1962 brought the first cold war—Stalin's cold war—to an end. The East-West conflict would continue but would never be quite the same.

———

Throughout this protracted conflict, Khrushchev was the driving force. He has been romanticized in the West and more recently inside the Soviet Union as the forerunner of Gorbachev, the first de-Stalinizer, the first reformer. His foreign policy adventures are rationalized. Thus the Cuban crisis is explained as an effort to save Castro from the designs of the CIA; the confrontation that followed was a misunderstanding on both sides.

The record, of course, is radically different. Khrushchev was a crude practitioner of ruthless power politics, a dangerous gambler who brought the world close to war. He was belligerent; he recklessly exploited the most sensitive and dangerous point of conflict—Berlin—and then ventured onto even more dangerous ground by invading the western hemisphere. He encouraged wars of liberation, funded and armed some of them, proposed wrecking the UN, constantly taunted and threatened the West, and boasted of Soviet strength and western weaknesses. His threats were frequent and indiscriminate, and only his reputation as something of a buffoon saved him from having his threats taken at face value. He was the father of diplomacy by rocket coercion, and much of the buildup of Soviet military power in the 1960s was founded on Khrushchev's initiatives.

For three decades he was Stalin's loyal sycophant. He was a braggart and a bully. He ordered the tanks into Budapest and condoned the murder of Imre Nagy. He sowed the seeds of the Brezhnev doctrine and, of course, built the Wall in Berlin and put the missiles in Cuba.

It is true, however, that he never pressed these forays too far, and at a crucial moment he pulled back in Cuba. He fought against the extremely dangerous proposals by Mao to test the capitalist system by war. And he experimented with loosening the Soviet empire in Eastern Europe. It is also true that he had the courage to overthrow Beria and the power of the secret police—one of the fundamental of all post-Stalin changes. And, of course, he attacked Stalin and his crimes, but he never questioned the fundamentals of Stalin's political system, and he certainly never intended to tear it down. When he began to press his political and economic reforms too far, his colleagues removed him and did so with surprising ease, in part because of the humiliation brought on by his foreign policy. Had his external policies been more prudent he might have survived and perhaps pursued some of his internal reforms, in which case the history of the Soviet Union might have taken a far different turn.

Berlin was a ready-made pressure point for Khrushchev. No western position was more vulnerable, and in the decade since Stalin's blockade the vulnerability of the isolated outpost had sharply increased. It was still 110 miles behind the lines. But it was no longer a desperate beleaguered city with little to lose. The idea of supplying a large modern city by air was no longer feasible. In 1948 the clash was between the occupying powers, and this imposed certain limits on all sides. A decade later the situation had changed: there were two German states, and East Germany was in physical control over the routes of access. The Russian presence at the various checkpoints was nominal. The West insisted that its rights in Berlin were unconditional and that the entire city was still under occupation and was administered as a whole, in both the eastern and western sectors. In practice, however, the East German government was administering East Berlin—the suburb of Pankow was the seat of the East German government.

Khrushchev shrewdly exploited this new situation. He did not threaten to cut off Berlin, as Stalin had. Instead, he proposed that the western powers leave, give up their occupation rights, and turn West Berlin into a "free city," under UN administration if need be. He did not threaten to block the access routes but to transfer their control to East Germany, and to do so by the seemingly legal vehicle of signing a German peace treaty. The West could then deal with East Germany, a regime the West had steadfastly refused to recognize.

All of this was not set forth in reasoned diplomatic discourse but in bombastic speeches and polemical messages interspersed with violent threats of war. Khrushchev had the reputation of a clever tactician. But in the Berlin crisis his manner and methods worked against him.

There is little doubt that the western powers would have negotiated a new arrangement for controlling Berlin access had Khrushchev not challenged their basic rights so blatantly. Western occupation rights in Berlin were a particularly sensitive area. There was little legal documentation for these rights and for the various forms of access. They rested on an exchange of letters between Stalin and Truman, and between the two local commanders in 1945. But Washington and London, however, insisted that their rights were inherent in the defeat of Germany and its unconditional surrender. It is not impossible that Khrushchev could have negotiated a document ending the occupation in Berlin and even decreeing a state of peace in Germany. But to threaten to do so unilaterally and impose the consequences on his old wartime allies could only produce a growing resentment and resistance.

Nevertheless, his challenge was an insidious one. Any change in the status of Berlin naturally affected the larger German problem. Theoretically Berlin was being held in trust for the German people until unification would permit its restoration as the national capital. Thus any change in Berlin's status suggested an undermining of this commitment to the German people, and consequently an undermining of faith in Adenauer's policy of remaining firmly tied to the West until unification. For this reason, the West immediately challenged Khrushchev's concept of a separate agreement on Berlin outside the context of a German settlement. Khrushchev thereupon produced a draft peace treaty in which Germany would become neutral, while armed, but without any foreign forces stationed on its territory. The wartime victors, however, would retain rights of intervention to prevent certain "hostile" acts.

Thus the West faced a dilemma. It could negotiate on unfavorable terms, or confront the results of a Soviet unilateral peace treaty. Negotiating on unconditional rights was unpalatable, but to provoke a war crisis over which official stamped which document at the Helmstedt checkpoint on the autobahn seemed ludicrous. Dulles recognized this at once and devised a clever formula by which the East Germans would be treated merely as the "agents" of the Soviets. It was a transparent dodge, but at least it was an effort to defuse the threat. The alternative was to force the way through the checkpoints and press down the autobahn. One proposal from General Norstad, then the American commander in NATO, was to use a division to rescue any blocked truck convoy. Eisenhower disdainfully pointed out that a division was either too much or too little.

The West reluctantly decided to negotiate. To talk the crisis to death became the basic western strategy throughout—to keep negotiating until the various deadlines and threats evaporated. The western powers challenged Khrushchev's original assertion that their rights in Berlin came from the Potsdam agreement (an erroneous claim in any case). They reminded Khrushchev that solving Berlin without addressing the larger problem of Germany was obviously inconsistent. They proposed to negotiate, to convene the four-power foreign ministers, and even hinted at a summit. But at Eisenhower's insistence they argued that they could not negotiate under duress, that the six-month deadline had to be withdrawn. This proved to be a far more successful strategy than seemed likely at first. It appealed to Khrushchev's combative spirit to engage in political arguments and diplomatic debates. An intricate game developed in which Khrushchev's threat was indeed softened and virtually withdrawn by him but negotiations began more or less on Soviet terms. The West, after all, had no interest in altering the status quo in Berlin, which could not fail to have an unfavorable impact in Germany. But by March 1959 the West entered into negotiations with the Soviets on this very question.

One reason for this was that the western camp was badly divided when it came to the question of Germany, especially when called upon to risk a major confrontation over the recognition of East Germany. The British prime minister, Harold Macmillan, proved to be the weakest link. He and Eisenhower were close; they had worked together during the war. Like Churchill, Macmillan had an American mother, a point Eisenhower always counted in his favor. After Suez, Macmillan had rebuilt relations with Washington, especially as Dulles's influence receded (after he became ill with terminal cancer). Macmillan was well liked by Americans. David Bruce, the American ambassador in London under Kennedy, described him: "At times he gives the impression of being shot through with Victorian languor. . . . But this is no mean man. . . . He has charm, politeness, dry humor, self-assurance, a vivid sense of history, dignity, and character."

But during the Berlin crisis Macmillan became more and more alarmed. At the outset of the crisis, he expressed his fears in a note to his ambassador in Moscow, wondering whether Khrushchev's "megalomania" might turn out to be the most perilous point in a confused picture, whether Khrushchev could "do foolish things as Hitler did." Moreover, Macmillan was facing a general election in 1959 and was embarking on the delicate task of negotiating Britain's entry into Europe, which meant confronting de Gaulle. He needed to overcome centuries of British resistance to a European commitment. But to do so in the name of defending Germany was impossible. Thus he desperately sought a way out, to the point that he decided to go to Moscow, and during his meetings he made major concessions to Khrushchev, causing a near-panic in Bonn.

While in Moscow, Macmillan was personally humiliated by Khrushchev's boorish behavior, in rudely canceling meetings, keeping the prime minister waiting for two days. But Macmillan did succeed in having the ultimatum set aside and stimulated a proposal for a foreign ministers' meeting (by conceding that European disengagement could also be on the agenda, thus further alarming Adenauer).

De Gaulle was much firmer throughout in confronting the Soviets, but on the substance he implicitly supported Macmillan. De Gaulle's view was that the division of Germany had to continue until a general European settlement was reached, and this clearly was not on the horizon. De Gaulle favored the status quo but was not prepared to run risks to preserve it in a pristine form. He urged the West Germans to recognize the Oder-Neisse border with Poland to appease the Soviets.

For de Gaulle, beneath the Soviet facade was Russia. He once asked Eisenhower whether he believed that after two world wars, Peter the Great would have settled the Russian frontiers any differently than Stalin. Technical agreements on armaments might have some value, de Gaulle conceded, but they would be reached by the two superpowers, thus perpetuating the two blocs. France, on the other hand, wanted a rapprochement between European nations. Promoting the rapprochement would be France's role. If Khrushchev spoke of keeping Germany divided, de Gaulle would not contradict him, because he saw no satisfactory future for a reunified Germany, except in the context of a general European settlement.

Eisenhower was also surprised by Macmillan and complained about him to Dulles and to his own staff. He was treated to constant complaints from Adenauer about Macmillan. Adenauer, Eisenhower concluded, had developed an almost psychopathic fear of what he considered to be British weakness. Despite Eisenhower's own worries, he reassured Adenauer that Macmillan stood foursquare with the western allies but because of internal problems had to "tread a very careful path." For his part the president had become uneasy with Dulles's legalistic strategy of presenting differences with the Soviets as a lawyer might present a brief. He confided to his diary that he sensed a distancing between his approach and Dulles's: "I sometimes question the practice of becoming a sort of international prosecuting attorney in which I lay out all of the things that I intend to prove before the jury. . . ."

Dulles did not survive to manage the Berlin crisis. He died of cancer in May 1959, and by then he had already been replaced by Christian Herter. Thereafter, Eisenhower assumed more and more of the tactical control of the crisis. (One can only wonder how Dulles would have managed the U-2 affair; certainly no worse than Herter and Eisenhower himself.) In any case, in mid-1959 the president began to see a personal meeting with Khrushchev as one way out—an approach not dissimilar from Macmillan's. But Eisenhower continued to insist on the withdrawal of the Berlin deadline as a precondition.

Khrushchev's deadline had been softened to permit the opening of the Geneva foreign ministers' conference, but the concept of a time limit for the talks had not been formally disavowed. The atmosphere for the Geneva negotiations was scarcely auspicious. The foreign ministers began meeting shortly after one of Khrushchev's more strident speeches, in which he said that the Soviet forces were not in Germany to play games; if the West tried to force its way through to Berlin by air, land, or water, it would mean "war." If the situation was not resolved, the USSR would sign a separate peace treaty.

The conference turned out to be a bizarre affair. Both German states were represented at the meetings, but their representatives were assigned to side tables. The West found itself negotiating on issues it considered nonnegotiable, in the presence of a state it refused to acknowledge, and under the duress of an implicit ultimatum it had insisted be withdrawn. One can only wonder whether this was not a strategic mistake that led to drastic consequences later.

The conference began with the West arguing that Berlin could not be discussed in isolation from the question of German unity. The Soviets countered that Berlin could only be discussed separately. Under western pressure, the Soviet position finally shifted and tied the status of Berlin to the signature of a peace treaty with both German states, that is, not with a unified Germany. Thus the Soviet negotiators turned the western concept to their advantage. The West, for its part, facing the harsh terms of a Soviet peace treaty with a divided Germany, switched and adopted the old Soviet position—that Berlin should be resolved separately from the German issues. This reversal of positions caused the French foreign minister to comment that neither side knew what the other was talking about—an apt description.

In any case, the conference began to founder, and something had to be done lest Khrushchev be forced to revive his deadline. The result was an invitation to Khrushchev to visit the United States. This seemed a shrewd move at the time, appealing to Khrushchev's ego and simultaneously making it difficult for him to carry out any threats of unilateral action. It turns out that it was unintentional—that Eisenhower had not known his subordinates would proceed to issue an actual invitation; he had been speculating about inviting Khrushchev but without having decided to do so.

Khrushchev accepted, of course, and his visit did de-escalate the crisis. While little of substance was agreed, it did set the stage for a full-scale summit meeting in Paris. Eisenhower had hoped for an early summit, but de Gaulle intervened and insisted that Khrushchev meet with him separately beforehand. The summit was delayed until May 1960, a U.S. election year. Meanwhile, a thaw was setting in. There was even speculation after Khrushchev's visit to Camp David that the cold war was over: one could hear the ice of the cold war cracking, wrote one newspaper.

In fact, the situation was quite different. Gradually it began to dawn on both sides that the summit was likely to fail. Khrushchev's basic demands for a change in Berlin and a German peace treaty had not been altered. The West could not accommodate these demands without risking the collapse of its entire alliance policy. It was late for facile formulas that might paper over the confrontation. On both sides there was a tendency to hedge against failure by speaking out to establish a record. Khrushchev began to bluster. In the United States, Vice President Nixon, Undersecretary of State Douglas Dillon, and Secretary Christian Herter, Dulles's successor, spoke aggressively in defense of western rights in Berlin. More and more it seemed that both sides had decided there was no chance for progress. And then suddenly came the announcement in Moscow that a U.S. reconnaissance plane, the U-2, had been shot down over the Soviet interior, near Sverdlovsk. After Washington denied any spy flights, Khrushchev revealed that the pilot, Francis Gary Powers, had been captured alive. The summit was in jeopardy, especially after Eisenhower took personal responsibility for the incident, thus challenging Khrushchev.

Both the original American denial and the subsequent admission were blunders. The entire affair was badly handled, but it was Khrushchev who drove matters into a new confrontation. He demanded an American apology but went to Paris to open the summit conference accompanied by his minister of defense, Marshal of the Soviet Union Rodion Malinovsky (who looked the part). At the first meeting, Khrushchev made the same demands for an apology. Eisenhower was furious, and for all practical purposes the summit failed before it began (Khrushchev insisted that the first encounter was "preliminary" and that the summit as such had not begun). Macmillan virtually collapsed and appealed for some kind of compromise—a "solemn dirge" from Macmillan was de Gaulle's description. Even Eisenhower was tempted to find a way out, but de Gaulle intervened to say that he would not permit Eisenhower to make concessions, which suited Eisenhower in any case. The summit was never reconvened. Macmillan later wrote in his memoirs that there was nothing he could do except to conceal as best he could "my disappointment amounting almost to despair—so much attempted, so little achieved."

Khrushchev was at his most obnoxious and belligerent in his final press conference in Paris, with Marshal Malinovsky in full dress uniform at his side (the equivalent of putting a loaded six-shooter on the table during a poker game, one observer described it). Khrushchev threatened nearly everyone (a Hitlerian performance, the British press described it). And there was growing alarm when he indicated that he would be stopping in Berlin on his way back to Moscow; it was believed that once in Berlin he would announce a separate peace treaty, as he had been threatening, and the Berlin crisis would reach its climax. In Berlin, he did nothing of the sort, but meekly suggested waiting for the next president. De Gaulle commented that having moved "heaven and earth to intimidate everyone," Khrushchev now adopted an attitude of moderation.

KENNEDY AND THE
WALL

"**O**ur most somber talks were on the subject of Germany and Berlin," President Kennedy reported to the American people on his meeting with Nikita Khrushchev in Vienna in June 1961. The new crisis was to prove more than somber. It became the most intensive and dangerous episode since the outbreak of the Korean War.

Khrushchev once again delivered an ultimatum, again for a six-month deadline. But this time it was handed to John Kennedy personally by the Soviet dictator in what amounted to a humiliation for the eager new president. For the first time, each side resorted to military moves to intimidate the other. Moscow was to explode the largest nuclear weapon in history in an orgy of nuclear blackmail. At one point American and Soviet tanks confronted each other along the narrow confines of Friedrichstrasse at Checkpoint Charlie in West Berlin.

Strangely, however, the crisis abated, but only after Khrushchev had safeguarded his puppet regime behind a wall of barbed wire and the West had demonstrated once again that it was not prepared to challenge the Soviet sphere. The rules of the cold war still applied, but not for long. The Berlin Wall seemed to be a bold thrust by Khrushchev, but in fact it was an admission of failure, and it led inexorably to Cuba.

=====

Khrushchev's resumption of threats to Berlin after his meeting with President Kennedy in Vienna (June 1961) touched off a new panic in East Berlin. The flow of refugees became a torrent—more than two thousand on a single day in early August—and threatened to bring down the East German regime. Khrushchev's choice was either to block West Berlin, reviving the Stalin crisis of 1948, or to seal off East Berlin from West Berlin and from the surrounding Soviet zone of Germany. He eventually chose the Wall, which was the least risky, and turned out to be the most effective.

Before the Wall, tensions were accentuated by Kennedy's own performance, especially the wide publicity he gave to the brutality of his encounter with Khrushchev. His own ominous final comment to Khrushchev that it was going to be a "cold winter" was quickly leaked to the press. Kennedy seemed obsessed with Khrushchev's conduct in Vienna. He reported on it at length to Macmillan, when he stopped in London immediately after leaving Vienna. Macmillan, who had been subjected to a humiliating confrontation with Khrushchev two years earlier, found Kennedy concerned and even surprised by the "brutal frankness and confidence" of the top Soviet leader. The president was "impressed and shocked." Macmillan's description of Kennedy's reaction: "It was rather like somebody meeting Napoleon [at the height of his power] for the first time."

Back in Washington, Kennedy read portions of the summit transcripts to his friends, including newsmen. He organized task forces to prepare for contingencies, including military action, and prepared an alarming report for the public. Most worrisome, the impression began to circulate that Kennedy had been intimidated by Khrushchev. And Kennedy did say that he thought the Russians believed they had the upper hand, would not make any concession, and were no longer afraid of the American reaction. In the company of older, more experienced hands, especially Acheson, this moment of near-panic began to subside. Ironically, the debate in Washington took quite a different course: whether a strong reaction was really justified, and whether it would not kill the chances for a negotiation.

Kennedy's basic error was in his concept of the issue. He saw the conduct of East-West relations in a classic postwar context: what was required was first a posture of firmness, but then a willingness to negotiate; this formula would lead to progress. He hoped that "small breakthroughs" could lead to larger ones. As Theodore Sorenson put it, "brick by brick a détente could be built." This was a textbook logic that might have worked in another time and with another leader (Gorbachev, for example). But Kennedy (and some of his advisers) never quite accepted that Khrushchev was playing a game for much higher stakes. As Churchill said of Stalin, Khrushchev did not want war, but he wanted the fruits of victory.

Kennedy was in some measure the unfortunate victim of his erudite and brilliant advisers. Just before Kennedy's inauguration, Khrushchev had delivered a long speech, ostensibly reporting on the international meeting of communist parties held the month before in Moscow. In fact, the speech was also a long attack on the Chinese, but delivered in that Aesopian language that communists employ. Thus, Khrushchev boasted of Soviet support for "just" wars of national liberation, but he put it in a context that allowed him to attack Mao for his radical left-wing adventurism. At this time, in early 1961, there was still major skepticism in the West about the Sino-Soviet split. Many experts, especially in the U.S. government, were convinced that it was no more than a "family quarrel." In any case it could not be counted on as a factor in Soviet conduct. This was quite misleading. Khrushchev was more and more obsessed with the Chinese challenge. He was heading for a major confrontation with Peking and had already taken drastic steps that were unknown in the West, such as withdrawing all assistance to the Chinese nuclear weapons program.

The Khrushchev speech caused something of a sensation. On its face it seemed a declaration of war against the West, and this is how Kennedy and his advisers read it. Kennedy ordered the text circulated to his administration, and he read portions aloud to his cabinet.

With this ominous speech as a background, Kennedy, upon taking office, adopted very strong rhetoric—pay any price, bear any burden, etc. And it may well be that Khrushchev's declaration led the administration to read some early moves quite incorrectly. When the communist forces in Laos stepped up the fighting, it was interpreted in terms of Khrushchev's vow to prosecute wars of liberation. The Soviets did indeed support the communist faction in Laos, but in order to compete with the Chinese, not out of a doctrinal commitment. Kennedy thought it was a major challenge, and this interpretation led him to take up Laos with Khrushchev at Vienna. The Soviet leader seemed uninterested and even puzzled by Kennedy's concern. A subsequent compromise in Laos arranged by Averell Harriman did not help; it must have convinced Khrushchev that there was no resolve behind American rhetoric.

Kennedy was on the defensive, but fearful that he would be seen as too soft in the face of this new and dangerous challenge he perceived emanating from Moscow. But he was not content to take a strong position and dig in to defend it. Rather, he was intrigued by the chance of some progress through diplomacy and negotiations. He saw Berlin as susceptible to a negotiated solution, and therefore he was strongly inclined to an early summit. His analysis was buttressed by many of the experts (Bohlen and Thompson), who also urged a summit. Thus he conducted the summit as if the outcome would depend on the participants' debating skills. Throughout the Berlin crisis he badgered his advisers for ideas for a settlement. Even after the confrontation with Khrushchev in Vienna, he gradually returned to the idea that what was lacking was the right formula. He was perfectly willing to adopt the recommendations of the hard-line group advising him, as far as announcing greater military readiness and a buildup of forces. But he could not let matters rest with that response. He wanted to probe for talks, and in this sense he encouraged rather than discouraged Khrushchev.

Nevertheless, Kennedy's approach was not very much different from the Eisenhower-Dulles strategy of stalling by means of negotiations. Of course, Dulles never believed that Berlin could be resolved, and on his deathbed he urged Eisenhower to stand firm. Kennedy, however, believed in negotiations not to gain time but seek some solution, even if an interim one. For almost a year he was encouraged in this by the State Department. Secretary Rusk was instinctively dubious but saw negotiations as a safer course than the hard-line confrontation urged by his former chief Dean Acheson (who had been enlisted by Kennedy as a special adviser).

Personalities are important, and the changeover from Eisenhower to Kennedy made a difference. Eisenhower brought great experience to the White House as well as a sense of proportion. He was not impressed by Khrushchev; after all, Eisenhower had worked closely with Churchill and Roosevelt. Though he was quick to anger, Eisenhower was remarkably disciplined and acted in cold blood, a trait he had learned from MacArthur when he served as his aide for a decade. Eisenhower was not good at diplomatic subtleties or lengthy debates, and his language was often too crude for the nuances of politics; this was not surprising if one knew anything of life in the old army. His instincts were remarkably good, and his solutions to problems were usually solidly grounded in common sense and a well-developed feeling for what the average American would think.

Kennedy, of course, was much younger and was the product of a different background and social circumstance. He was far better educated, well-spoken, more polished, with a social grace and sense of humor that made him almost a cult figure. He was naturally at ease in personal encounters and in the company of great men, by virtue of his parents' political status and connections. Khrushchev's crude behavior would have been understood by the president's father, Joseph Kennedy, or his grandfather, Honey Fitz, who had prospered in Irish politics, but for the new president the confrontation was something of a shock.

Kennedy was quick and could be forceful. His problem may have been that he knew too much, saw too many angles, and wanted to exhaust too many options before acting. These characteristics betrayed him in the Bay of Pigs. Because of an instinctive skepticism about the project he kept scaling it back to satisfy various opinions and critics, without quite realizing that he was jeopardizing the entire enterprise. His innate respect for the leaders of the eastern establishment, including the CIA director, Allen Dulles, inhibited him from questioning the operation. That same respect for the professional military kept him from urging them to review and reshape the operation for a certain victory. His confidence in the establishment was shaken by the Bay of Pigs, but this led him in Berlin to question the book solution of standing firm as proposed by the Acheson wing of his advisers.

The difference between Eisenhower and Kennedy also lay in the strategic circumstances.

First, there was the simple passing of time. Kennedy took office almost three years after Khrushchev's original ultimatum on Berlin, and over three years after the Sputnik was supposed to have changed the balance of power. Yet Khrushchev had nothing to show for his threats or his diplomacy. And at home he was being driven into more radical measures of de-Stalinization to discredit his conservative opponents. It became a debating point in the West that something should be done for Khrushchev in Berlin to save his face and strengthen his hand against the "Stalinists." Thus American supporters of this view, such as Senators Fulbright and Mansfield, argued that Khrushchev had the "right" to change the situation in Berlin and the United States ought to accommodate him—for example, by creating a free city for all of Berlin. Kennedy did not agree with the thesis of helping Khrushchev, but he did not discourage such trial balloons.

This was a faulty perception of Khrushchev's internal predicament. There were real issues between Khrushchev and the Stalinists, and there were real Stalinists, both in the old guard and among Khrushchev's own protégés, as would become evident after he was overthrown. In 1961, however, the issues in the Kremlin were not so much Khrushchev's foreign policy as his radical domestic reforms that the bureaucracy feared would lead to a diminished role for the party. And to make matters more complicated, the Soviet dispute with Mao worsened. The major international communist gathering in late 1960 had failed to repair the breach and had revealed that the Chinese were gathering support, from Albania, Romania, Cuba, and Vietnam. The Chinese were particularly snide in their comments about Khrushchev's cowardly behavior at the time of the U-2. Khrushchev was more and more determined to show the Chinese that he could handle the imperialists.

The second and related difference between the Eisenhower period and

Kennedy's was a strengthening of the Western position compared to 1957–58, when much of the world believed that the Soviets were in the ascendancy. Then the West was on the defensive, striving to catch up in strategic missiles. Even Kennedy had campaigned on this premise in 1960. But after taking office, he came to realize that this was not the case, and gradually it became clear that the Soviets were behind the United States in nuclear weaponry. (At Vienna, Khrushchev said to Kennedy that in "his heart" he believed the Soviet Union was superior, but that he would settle for parity.) This issue was important to the dispute with China, for Mao argued that the "East Wind prevailed over the West Wind," and the Soviets should therefore go on to a major offensive against the United States. Khrushchev never liked advice from China, and he was beginning to realize that the East Wind was in fact not prevailing.

Thus Khrushchev arrived for the Vienna summit under pressure to act. He had in his pocket a memorandum on Berlin reviving the deadline (the end of 1961). That memorandum set forth a maximum Soviet position—a free city and a peace treaty with a divided Germany. There had been some speculation that Khrushchev might be open to an interim agreement on Berlin as a face saver. He had hinted at such. But by June, Khrushchev had given up on gaining anything substantial from the West. Only pressures would pay off. Therefore, the USSR quickly released this private threat after the end of the summit.

Much has been made over Kennedy's performance at the summit. Supposedly, he failed to rebut Khrushchev adequately and appeared cowed by the Soviet dictator's tough style. Tongue-tied, George Kennan commented. Kennedy's conduct, coming soon after the fiasco of the Bay of Pigs, allegedly convinced Khrushchev that he could move against the United States. (This interpretation was confirmed by Soviet officials discussing the Cuban missile crisis in 1989.) The problem with this analysis is that it ignores evidence that even before the Bay of Pigs, Khrushchev had made it clear that he would move to revive the Berlin crisis. In April he said as much to Walter Lippmann, who reported it in ominous colors in his column. According to Lippmann, Khrushchev conveyed an urgency about Berlin because he needed first of all to consolidate the East German regime, and second because he had to act before the Germans acquired nuclear weapons. Lippmann was sobered by his encounter, mainly because he did not detect any "bluff" in it.

Moreover Khrushchev said the same thing about Berlin to Ambassador Thompson in a long dialogue in the Siberian city of Novosibirsk. This is not to say that Kennedy's demeanor did not count in Khrushchev's estimate of how far he could press. In his talks with Lippmann before the Bay of Pigs, Khrushchev had seemed to write off Cuba as an inevitable victim of the United States. Lippmann concluded that in Khrushchev's book it was normal for a great power to undermine an unfriendly government within its own sphere of interest. If this was Khrushchev's mind-set—and it rings true—then Kennedy's error was not that he staged the operation but that he failed to intervene to save it. To be sure, in his memoirs Khrushchev is condescending; he wrote that he "felt sorry" for Kennedy, who had seemed to show his disappointment in their last private chat in Vienna.

Perhaps more important was something Kennedy said in that final private conversation. Kennedy implied he would not interfere in the Soviet sphere, meaning East Berlin, but could not tolerate interference in the western sphere. Khrushchev could have read this as a signal that he would have a free hand in such an action as putting up the Wall. Kennedy then implied the same in public, when he listed the three basic elements of the American position: to maintain the American presence in West Berlin, to guarantee free access to the city, and to guarantee the freedom and viability of West Berlin.

Notably absent was any guarantee of freedom of movement between East and West Berlin. This was heard with alarm by the mayor of West Berlin, Willy Brandt. Kennedy's former assistant Theodore Sorensen notes in his biography of Kennedy that the Wall did not "interfere with the three basic objectives the West had long stressed."

Finally, a few days after the end of the summit in Vienna, the East German communist leader Walter Ulbricht was busy denying rumors of a wall in Berlin, and this probably means that the subject had already been discussed with Khrushchev.

In short, there is a good chance that by the time of the Vienna summit Khrushchev had decided on his course of action—to restart the Berlin crisis and press it hard. Kennedy's error may have been in inspiring the idea that sealing off East Berlin would not be challenged.

From the end of the Vienna summit in early June 1961 through the middle of August was one of the most intense periods of the cold war. In effect, each side tried to intimidate the other. Kennedy sounded the alarm in a speech after the summit, coming very close to declaring a national emergency. He was influenced by Acheson, who concluded that the best posture was a tough one that might deter Khrushchev, whose aim was to test the West. Later, Rusk would regain control of policy and initiate negotiations, but not before the Berlin Wall.

Kennedy has been attacked by some historians for showing no signs of conciliation after Vienna, for adopting a military response, for calling for an additional $3 billion in defense funds, and for stressing a civil defense program. It is argued by revisionists that his strong speech of July 25 somehow forced Khrushchev's hand. But it must be remembered that by that time Khrushchev had already escalated. The first step was Khrushchev's release of his memorandum demanding a settlement by the end of the year. In his own report on the summit on June 15 he announced that the conclusion of a German peace treaty could no longer be put off, that "a peace settlement in Europe must be attained this year." In another speech on June 21, he warned: "If you really threaten us with war, we are not afraid of such a threat. If you do touch off a war, that will be suicide for you." Moreover, Khrushchev responded in one speech by appearing in his lieutenant general's uniform. We now also know from the reports of the Soviet spy Oleg Penkovsky that Khrushchev's threats were being taken seriously inside the Soviet hierarchy. There was some very worried talk among high-level Soviet military officers about Khrushchev's reckless behavior, and muttering that they were by no means prepared for the war he was threatening. Some of these reports were circulating in policymaking levels in Washington and adding to the growing alarm. This discontent in the Soviet high command may explain why shortly before putting up the Wall Khrushchev ordered the wartime conqueror of Berlin, Marshal Ivan Konev, out of retirement and put him in temporary command in Berlin.

At one point Khrushchev told the British ambassador that it would take only six atomic bombs to destroy England (nine for France). He warned "any state" that would be used as a springboard for an attack. In early July, Khrushchev announced that he was suspending the reduction in the Soviet armed forces that he had boasted of the preceding year, and would raise the Soviet defense budget. Shortly before the Wall was put up, he said in a speech that the western powers were pushing the world toward a dangerous divide and that "the emergence of the threat of an armed attack by imperialists on socialist states cannot be ignored."

But most terrifying was the resumption of nuclear testing in flat contradiction to his statement to Kennedy that the USSR would not be the first to break the test moratorium. Shortly after exploding a huge bomb (about sixty megatons), a month after putting up the Berlin Wall, he wrote to Nehru: "In all the postwar period the threat of war has never, perhaps, been felt as keenly as today."

All of this was intended to frighten the West, both before and after putting up the Wall—only a strip of barbed wire in the beginning. It began in the early hours of August 13, 1961. There had been some vague warnings in various intelligence channels and much speculation about what Khrushchev would do. Still, it was a surprise. It took Washington some time to organize its reaction, but in the end the decision was to do nothing. To use force to penetrate the barbed wire was quite feasible, but then what? How far would the United States go into East Berlin? This was the rationale, attributed to General Lucius Clay, for accepting the *fait accompli.* This had been implicit in the western position, but as it became clear a sense of shock spread in both West Germany and Berlin.

Adenauer reacted too calmly, and he came under political attack from the opposition. In the elections in September he suffered his first setback.

Thereafter he had to compromise in putting together a coalition government. The foreign ministry went to a Liberal Democrat, Gerhard Schroeder, who began to develop a new position on the German question. This new policy, called "little steps," gradually relaxed Bonn's rigid resistance to any manifestation of recognition of East Germany. Formerly, Adenauer's policy was to break relations with any government recognizing East Germany; but this was dropped for Yugoslavia, and then for some of the other Eastern European governments.

Thus Khrushchev's aims would be achieved: acceptance of East Germany and the Soviet sphere in the East would come, but not until Willy Brandt became chancellor in 1969. For Brandt, in 1961, when he was still mayor of West Berlin, the failure of Bonn as well as the western allies to act against the Wall was proof that the West could not be relied on to pursue German national aims; henceforth any German government would have to act on its own. When he became chancellor he adopted a new eastern policy.

This was in the future in the late summer of 1961. The Berlin crisis had reached a climax. East Berlin did not explode as some feared. There was a very dangerous moment in October when the United States brought tanks up to the Wall and the crossing point in the Friedrichstrasse as a show of force to support its right to travel unmolested into East Berlin. The Soviets countered with their own tanks but then withdrew, whereupon the American tanks were quickly withdrawn. In his memoirs Khrushchev takes credit for ending this mini-crisis on the advice of Marshal Konev, who telephoned him from Berlin.

The crisis ended with a whimper, not the bang many feared. Khrushchev relaxed his deadline once again. He had again failed to sign the long-threatened peace treaty with East Germany and failed to dislodge the western powers from Berlin. True, he had salvaged his East German ally, but in the process he had retreated from his larger goals. So the crisis faded, but it was not to end until Soviet missiles went into Cuba, one year later.

10

CONFRONTATION

In the spring of 1962, Nikita Khrushchev was embattled on almost every front. At home his struggle against the Stalinists had intensified, at his initiative. It took a dramatic turn in October 1961 at a party congress called to ratify the first new party program since 1919. Khrushchev launched a surprise attack on Stalinism and linked it to his old enemies (and old comrades) Molotov and Malenkov, whom he had defeated in 1957. They were resurrected so that Khrushchev could start a wider campaign against the entrenched party bureaucracy. The party elite were not all Stalinists, to be sure, but as a class they were conservative; they resisted Khrushchev's agricultural reforms and his shift in economic priorities from heavy industry to consumer goods. The priority to heavy industry, including defense production, was a hallowed tenet of Stalin's policies, and Khrushchev's most important economic and political target.

Khrushchev was a true believer, but he was also convinced that the Soviet system was stagnating and needed a complete reform. And by nature he was a tinkerer. His problem was that he had no clear idea of which reforms would work, so he experimented: some decollectivization of agriculture; some decentralization of economic planning; some diversion of resources from defense to consumption. None of it seemed to be very effective, and he became increasingly impatient and frustrated. He became convinced that the problem was inside the party itself; that the party needed to be thoroughly purged of its Stalinist past (as symbolized by the antiparty group of Malenkov, Molotov, and Kaganovich). In late 1961 he returned to de-Stalinization to break the party's resistance and, of course, to strengthen his own position.

Khrushchev was toying with an idea that would greatly intensify his struggle: a plan to split the party into two sections in order to encourage better performance and competition. One section would be responsible for industry and the other for agriculture. Thus in every region and at every level of the party hierarchy, there would be two party secretaries; it could only mean a built-in tension between the two sections and an invitation to conflict (this program would be implemented, but not until after the Cuban crisis).

At the party congress, Khrushchev arranged a dramatic demonstration. One delegate to the congress claimed that one night the spirit of Lenin had appeared to her; the spirit told her that he no longer wanted Stalin's body to lie next to him in the crypt. Late that night, on Halloween, earth-digging equipment carved out a new gravesite for Joseph Stalin near the Kremlin wall. His body was transferred from the Lenin mausoleum and the grave was then filled with concrete and a marble slab placed on the top; eventually a small bust would mark the site, just barely visible from Red Square. The next morning Moscow awoke to a new sign on the mausoleum that read, simply, "Lenin."

It was powerful symbolism, but it could not obscure the fact that Khrushchev's programs were in trouble. Per capita grain consumption in the USSR was less than in 1913. His experiment in Khazakhstan with the virgin-lands program had yielded impressive results at first (in 1956) but had gradually failed over the full five years (the official in charge of the virgin lands was Leonid Brezhnev). In his search for new ways to stimulate the peasants, Khrushchev was moving toward decentralization, giving greater authority to the farm managers. He was also searching for new funds for agriculture; he claimed that the sacrosanct heavy industry would yield new funds for the farming sector.

Consumer goods, as always in the Soviet Union, were in short supply, but the party bureaucracy was resisting the transfer of funds to consumer production. The "metal eaters," as Khrushchev called them, were still a powerful lobby, and they were thought to have the support of the military (and perhaps the KGB).

The denunciations at the party congress had focused on Molotov, who was accused of opposing the policy of peaceful coexistence. In the indictment, Molotov's views turned out to be similar to the Chinese party's position; he was a surrogate not only for the Stalinists but for the Chinese as well, another shrewd Khrushchev linkage, since the struggle with the Chinese had continued to worsen. To rebut the Chinese version of austere communism, Khrushchev had proclaimed to the party congress that the Soviet Union had begun building "full" communism.

But several important communist parties, including the Cuban and North Vietnamese, were not unsympathetic to Peking. The Chinese were implacable and relentless. After the Cuban missile crisis they attacked Khrushchev for "adventurism" in placing the missiles in Cuba, and for "capitulationism" in withdrawing them. One of Peking's chief antagonists was Deng Xiao-ping, who clashed with Khrushchev in a bitter argument in 1960 in Bucharest.

Chinese pressures added to the frustration over foreign policy, which had stalled after the Berlin Wall. Khrushchev had not produced the gains he had promised after the Sputnik launching in 1957. It had been three and a half years since his Berlin ultimatum. But the western allies were still firmly entrenched in their sectors of West Berlin. The United States, spurred by the threat of the Vienna summit and the Berlin Wall, was rearming. American missiles had been installed in Turkey, Italy, and Great Britain, in response to the war scare that followed the Sputnik. The missile gap portended by the Sputnik had never really materialized. By the fall of 1961 that fact had been confirmed by high-level American pronouncements. At the very moment when Khrushchev was banishing Stalin's corpse to the Kremlin wall, Washington was announcing that the missile gap had fully disappeared. Even worse for Khrushchev, a reverse missile gap was developing: the United States land- and sea-based missile program was surging ahead while the Soviet program was stalled, awaiting the second generation of missiles before embarking on a major deployment. This decision to wait for a better missile was to prove costly for Khrushchev. It meant that his earlier threats were in fact only a bluff. Eventually, well after Khrushchev had been removed from office, his decisions would pay off for his successors, who were able to deploy large ICBM forces within five years. But the lack of a larger force in 1962 weakened Khrushchev's position in the missile crisis.

Khrushchev needed a bold stroke to redress the strategic balance, and the solution was at hand: putting Soviet missiles in Cuba, where their range would threaten most of the eastern and southern United States. A force of, say, sixty missiles would put the Soviet Union on roughly the same level as the United States, with a potential for expanding the Cuban force quickly and cheaply.

We now know that by April 1962 Khrushchev was meeting with his principal colleagues to discuss such a deployment. Some in the Politburo were skeptical, and they doubted Castro's acquiescence. Gromyko, and apparently Mikoyan, raised the question of the American reaction but did not make it an issue. By June the question was settled; orders were issued to the general staff to draw up a list of equipment and manpower to be dispatched to Cuba. The deployment would include not only medium- and intermediate-range missiles (the SS-4 and SS-5), but light bomber aircraft (the Ilyushin-28), Soviet troops in large numbers (eventually almost forty thousand), and a rudimentary air defense system based on SA-2 interceptor missiles. A nuclear confrontation was in the making.

Such a confrontation was probably inevitable at some point in the cold war. By the early 1960s the nuclear balance had become an important component of the overall strategic balance. The nuclear arsenals of both sides were growing, and moreover, their composition was changing from slower, retaliatory weapons (bombers) to include both land- and sea-based ballistic missiles, as well as missiles deployed in Europe that gave some chance for a surprise attack. By late 1961, the United States could call on over three thousand nuclear weapons if given enough time to alert its forces. The Soviets had far fewer, probably no more than twenty-five missiles, and twelve hundred weapons at sea and some two hundred longer-range bombers. A new and crucial fact was being created: even if the United States attacked first with its missiles, some Soviet weapons would survive and could launch a devastating retaliation against American cities. This drove American strategists more and more in the direction of considering a first strike, not in cold blood but as a preemptive move to smash any anticipated Soviet attack. To be effective, however, such a preemptive strike had to concentrate on military targets to reduce any Soviet retaliation; perhaps as many as one thousand such targets were in the American plan.

But if Soviet missiles were to be placed in Cuba, a very short warning time from American cities, any preemptive strategy would become less and less feasible: missiles in Cuba would have to be attacked first by the United States, but this would provide a clear warning to the Soviet Union to disperse its bombers inside the USSR and its submarines at sea. This was a significant dimension of the Cuban venture. It would put the United States permanently under the threat of a short-warning attack and would undermine any counterstrategy designed to destroy Soviet nuclear forces. As nuclear strategy and forces became more sophisticated, such frightening scenarios would become more and more important in deciding about future nuclear forces.

Khrushchev was mesmerized by nuclear weapons. In January 1960 he had proclaimed that any future war would be a nuclear war, and therefore battleships and large armies were obsolescent. This enthusiasm for nuclear weapons brought him into conflict with the more traditional military officers, who continued to argue that there could be a war fought with conventional weapons. They also insisted that in any case the USSR had to be able to fight in either mode: conventional or nuclear. This in turn meant even heavier demands on a weak economy, and Khrushchev increasingly resented the military's claims. At Camp David in 1959 he had commiserated with Eisenhower about the demands of their respective military establishments.

Nevertheless, the professional Soviet military did take advantage of

Khrushchev to develop a doctrine that stressed peacetime preparations for actually fighting a nuclear war; rather than succumb to "bourgeois pessimism" that nuclear war would mean the end of civilization (Malenkov's heresy), they contended that given the right mix of strategic forces, nuclear war might be won. As the United States moved toward a policy stressing deterrence, the Soviets moved toward getting ready to fight a war, if need be. Missiles in Cuba fit this new tendency.

Khrushchev gave three different reasons for his missile gamble. First, he said that the only purpose of the missiles was to protect Cuba from an American invasion. This has remained the official rationale. But as one American scholar commented, it is "laughable." Soviet-Cuban relations were quite tense until late 1961; a prominent Cuban leader was purged for his pro-Soviet inclinations. Had Khrushchev been truly worried about Castro, then adding the strategic missiles to his buildup of Soviet forces was bound to change the nature of the confrontation. It is surprising how much the Kennedy administration did tolerate before the missiles were discovered. The presence of Soviet forces in large numbers, along with bomber aircraft, patrol boats, and even tanks, would have been a strong deterrent to any U.S. invading force.

Khrushchev recognized that this was a thin explanation, and later he added that the missiles would have protected Castro and "would have equalized what the West likes to call the balance of power." This was the explanation given to the ambassadors of the Warsaw Pact countries in Washington by Anastas Mikoyan immediately after the crisis. And it was the heart of the matter. The balance of power would have changed. There would soon have been a rough nuclear parity, and the world would have perceived it to be a new balance, psychologically and geopolitically. The Soviet Union would have demonstrated that it could intrude its power in the sphere of the United States with impunity. Khrushchev apparently intended to reveal the deployment after the midterm election in November 1962; then he would have reopened Berlin.

A third reason was also provided by Khrushchev: to even the score for U.S. missiles in Turkey. There is some testimony from Soviet officials that Khrushchev was first prompted to think about putting missiles in Cuba when reminded by Marshal Malinovsky, then the minister of defense, that the American missile base in Turkey was becoming operational.

It galled Khrushchev that the United States encircled the USSR with its bases. And this was the deeper meaning of the crisis: the effort to force a U.S. recognition of equal Soviet geopolitical rights to the same global status enjoyed by Americans. This motive tied the Cuban crisis back to Stalin's cold war insistence that the West had to accept fully the Soviet Union and its empire. The visceral Soviet feeling of inferiority would be wiped out by the Cuban base. Then America would also be under the gun. Ironically, it was this aspect that made a settlement possible. If the United States could retreat from Turkey, then the USSR could do the same in Cuba.

President Kennedy commented early in the crisis that the Soviets were seeking to close the debate with China, create a position of strength for reopening the Berlin issues, and deal a major blow to the United States (a sound appraisal). Berlin was the hostage in this crisis; if the United States moved against Cuba, Khrushchev would strike back in some manner at Berlin—or so the reasoning went in Washington. President Kennedy, in his speech revealing the crisis (October 22), warned that an attack "on Berlin would be an attack on the United States"—one of the most sweeping American commitments in the cold war and, given the circumstances, one of the most dangerous.

Nuclear weapons made the crisis automatically dangerous, but two other factors enhanced the sense of peril. First was the secrecy in which Khrushchev had proceeded, the deceit of Khrushchev and other officials in both denying the fact of the missile deployment and sending assurances to Kennedy that no crisis was imminent. Second, the deployment seemed to flaunt the cold war rules. These rules—unwritten, of course—suggested that each side would respect the sphere of the other. Kennedy, in his opening speech, summed it up precisely:

"This sudden, clandestine decision to station strategic weapons for the first time outside the Soviet Union [was] a deliberately provocative and unjustified change in the status quo."

When confronted with the fact that the United States had done the same thing with its missiles in Turkey (though openly and publicly), Kennedy commented that "that was five years ago." In other words, some rules of the game were being developed in the cold war. The United States had not challenged the Berlin Wall, and Khrushchev had not challenged German access to West Berlin. Now, in Cuba, the pattern had been crudely broken—and clandestinely. That is what made it a crisis of fundamental importance for the conduct of the cold war.

McGeorge Bundy, President Kennedy's national security adviser, once commented that forests have been felled to make the paper for the books and articles analyzing the Cuban missile crisis. Most of that analysis has been on the operational conduct of the crisis on each side: the American side has benefited by the public access to a great deal of documentation and oral history on Kennedy's handling of the crisis. More recently, some Soviet sources have become available that add a few nuances and insights to Khrushchev's conduct.

Soviet sources confirm that Khrushchev was seeking to change the balance of power, as he admitted after the crisis. It was to be the first step toward strategic parity, as two Soviet officials put it. Surprisingly, however, these same Soviet sources dismissed the question of Berlin as a cold war "game"—of a different character than the Cuban confrontation. This is more difficult to accept, since there is other evidence from the period that suggested Khrushchev would exploit the Cuban missiles to reopen the Berlin issue after the November elections. In any case, this is what President Kennedy thought.

Of special interest is a Soviet confirmation that Khrushchev did, in fact, believe that Kennedy was "too young, too intelligent, and too weak"; former Kennedy administration figures naturally balk at this implication, but it comes from Soviet sources who were aides to Khrushchev (Fyodor Burlatsky and Georgy Shakhnarazov). It is nevertheless difficult to believe that such a risky venture was based on Khrushchev's instinctive personal assessment of his opponent. But it does point up the importance of personalities, even though the cold war had a certain inexorable logic of its own. It is also a reminder that one side is apt to project its view into the mind of the other. In 1962, American analysts could not conceive that Khrushchev would take such a losing gamble as the Cuban venture, while most Soviet officials did not think the risks were all that great or that the reaction would be that severe. And those in Moscow who feared a crisis lacked the courage to contest Khrushchev.

In the end, Khrushchev paid a high price for his rash venture. He found that he could not threaten Berlin without advancing to the very brink of war, and he could not threaten nuclear war without risking the destruction of his country. So he retreated.

During the crisis both sides were extremely nervous and apprehensive that matters might swirl out of control. There was justification for such fears. During the crisis inadvertent events intruded: the shootdown of the American U-2 over Cuba, and the entry into Soviet airspace of a reconnaissance plane in the Far East. But the most important lessons of Cuba are not in the detail, but in the broader strategic consequences. The first and perhaps most durable consequence was—strangely—a reduction in the fear of nuclear war. Having learned that nuclear war was possible, both sides were sobered. It is no accident that after the crisis there were agreements that regulated nuclear conduct: the establishment of the first hot line for passing emergency messages (one Soviet message had taken several hours to deliver in the Cuban crisis); the agreement to terminate nuclear testing in the atmosphere and under water. The public outcry against atmospheric testing would have forced the same result, but the Cuban crisis was the catalyst. Accordingly, there was a general feeling that nuclear war—which for a few days had seemed possible—now was less likely.

On the other hand, the crisis convinced many on both sides that military hardware was important. Even if a nuclear exchange was highly unlikely, Cuba nevertheless had demonstrated that the side that struck first might have an advantage. A prominent Soviet official pointedly told his American counterpart that they would never suffer the same humiliation again, and the massive Soviet buildup in strategic weapons dates from this post-Cuban period (although the planning for the buildup had to have preceded it).

There was a related consequence. As both sides built offensive forces, each began to explore the idea of a strategic defense, which became known as the antiballistic missile (ABM). The Soviets even began to deploy a very limited system, and by 1966–67 the United States was moving in the same direction, albeit with more reservations about its effectiveness.

Another trend was the split that developed within the American establishment between the hawks and doves (the terms first appeared in this crisis). The core difference was whether the details of the strategic balance mattered, beyond a certain level of weaponry. The hawks argued that it mattered greatly, that the Soviet missiles had to be removed, and that the outcome was a triumph of American strategic superiority. Khrushchev had yielded because the ICBM balance was against him. The doves agreed the missiles could not be tolerated in Cuba, but argued that Cuba had been a victory without regard to any strategic balance, because both sides had the common sense to recognize that a nuclear exchange would be suicidal, and the United States had advantages on the spot, in the Carribbean. Thus the doves concluded that strategic nuances were not basically important: changes in the strategic balance could be digested, as long as a minimum deterrent existed.

This division in American policy circles was to grow as arms control negotiations with the USSR were finally begun in 1969, as the forces on both sides became more and more sophisticated, and as the consequent war-gaming became more and more arcane.

Thus the Soviet defeat in Cuba channeled the cold war into new avenues of competition—primarily in the field of strategic weapons, offensive and defensive. Of course, this had been an important feature before 1962, but after Cuba it became dominant. Both sides were reluctant to accept the balance of terror as a permanent characteristic of the cold war. What Khrushchev could not achieve by stealth, Brezhnev was to achieve by tenacity. A strategic parity was reached in the early 1970s. The older issues of the cold war from the Stalin period began to recede. Berlin was never again the source of high tension it had been in 1961–62. The bitterness over Eastern Europe began to dissipate as well. The Soviet intervention in Czechoslovakia in 1968 could easily have been a major crisis; for the West it proved to be an episode of far less importance than the Hungarian revolution of 1956.

It is conceivable that after Cuba the cold war might have been ended with a broader settlement. It is now known that the Cuban confrontation was terminated in part because of a last-minute bargain, in which the United States withdrew its Jupiter missiles from Turkey and the Soviets retreated from Cuba. Kennedy administration officials still adamantly deny that there was any explicit trade. They insist that the American missiles were to be withdrawn from Turkey in any case, and Khrushchev was only reminded of this fact through a conversation between Robert Kennedy and Ambassador Dobrynin. Nevertheless, this fact of intended withdrawal was emphasized to the Soviet side during the final maneuvering in the crisis. The evidence from the Soviet side is that Khrushchev interpreted the endgame as a bargain of Turkish for Soviet missiles. The Soviets quickly put this in writing, only to be warned that such a formal document would make the conclusion of the crisis impossible.

What is remarkable is not what happened in exact detail. It is no longer very important. But the substance of the implicit bargain suggests that it could have led to further, broader negotiations about spheres of influence and rules of nuclear conduct. The opening was never really explored by the American side. Perhaps these issues were not yet ripe for such an exploration: the Americans were too shamefaced to acknowledge that they had bargained away their allies' rights, and the Soviets were too weak to entertain any further dismantling of their strategic position.

Kennedy did provide an opportunity in a major conciliatory address in June 1963. The Soviet leaders responded with an initiative that led to the limited test ban treaty of July 1963. But more intriguing was Khrushchev's suggestion of a nonaggression treaty between NATO and the Warsaw Pact. It was dismissed as propaganda. Probably it had that purpose, but it is also possible that had it been tested something along the lines of the détente of the 1970s might have evolved in the early 1960s. But Khrushchev, like Stalin, paid a high price for his tactics of secrecy and deception. In December 1962, after the crisis, Kennedy said that "it is going to be some time before it is possible for us to come to any real understandings with Mr. Khrushchev."

Nevertheless, it was a victory for the United States. It was Kennedy's finest hour. Stalin's cold war ended in Cuba. Stalin had contended within a narrow sphere. Khrushchev broadened the battlefield well beyond Europe but the focal point was still Berlin and Germany. After the Cuban crisis the issues began to change: there was a more intense strategic competition in long-range weapons, and the focus of the conflict shifted to the third world (Vietnam). And, of course, the next phase was conducted by new leaders, for Kennedy and Khrushchev were gone within two years after their October crisis.

11

JOHNSON'S WAR

In July 1963 the two superpowers signed a treaty to end all nuclear testing in the atmosphere. It seemed then that despite the Cuban crisis the cold war might ease. This treaty was signed only nine months after the Cuban confrontation, and the change in the political climate in that brief period was dramatic. Within two years, however, the United States was at war in Indochina, fighting Vietcong and North Vietnamese forces supplied mainly by the USSR and supported by communist China. The cold war had shifted once again to a new front in Asia.

Was the Vietnam War the consistent application of the doctrines of containment practiced by every administration since Truman? Was the war a noble cause, as its supporters still argue twenty-five years later? Or was it an aberration, a departure from the main lines of American policy?

=====

The evidence suggests that the Johnson administration operated well within the mainstream of American foreign policy: to oppose the spread of communism, preferably by providing assistance to others, but by force if need be. The major decisions, however, were not the result of a mindless anticommunism. In most instances the decisions were debated—albeit in secret—and even fought over at some length. The men involved were intelligent, skilled, and experienced. They knew what they were doing.

In the first six months of 1965, the Johnson administration committed the power and prestige of the United States to the defense of South Vietnam. The first critical decision was to begin bombing North Vietnam. Initially the bombing was to be a signal, and thus could be regulated and calibrated. But within weeks the program had changed to a campaign to interdict supply lines to the south. Thus it had to be continued if it was to be effective. Yet it was treated in Washington as a bargaining chip, to be turned on and off in an effort to promote negotiations. This was an important mistake.

The second major decision, to commit American combat troops, was far more significant than the bombing. It was rationalized as a limited engagement to secure American base areas. Then the mission also changed; it became a limited combat mission. Once that corner was turned, the size and depth of the commitment had to grow; the momentum of war made this inexorable. The strategy of "search and destroy" implied a huge American force. But it also grew by design, and soon it was "Johnson's War."

Kennedy partisans claim that JFK would not have gone this far, but Johnson's partisans point to the advice of the president's men—Dean Rusk, Robert McNamara, and McGeorge Bundy—who were all Kennedy appointees, and they agreed on all of the initial commitments. There is a thread of legitimacy tying Eisenhower, Kennedy, and Johnson to Vietnam: the fear of the infamous dominoes that would inevitably fall if South Vietnam was lost. To be sure, there were key Kennedy advisers who doubted this central proposition, but as the government in Saigon fell into disarray and the insurgency grew, protecting the core of Indo-china, in Vietnam, became critical to the domino theory. Shortly before he was killed, President Kennedy was asked whether he subscribed to the domino theory. He answered, "I believe it . . . I believe it . . . China is so large . . . [Vietnam's fall] would also give the impression that the wave of the future in Southeast Asia was China and the communists. So I believe it."

The same general thesis was incorporated into policy decisions such as National Security Action Memorandum 288, of March 17, 1964:

"We seek an independent non-communist Vietnam. . . . Unless we can achieve this objective in South Vietnam, almost all of Southeast Asia will probably fall under Communist dominance (all of Vietnam, Laos and Cambodia), accommodate to Communism so as to remove effective U.S. and anti-Communist influence (Burma), or fall under domination of forces not now explicitly Communist but likely then to become so (Indonesia taking over Malaysia). Thailand might hold for a period without help but would be under grave pressure. Even the Philippines would become shaky, and the threat to India on the West, Australia and New Zealand to the South and Taiwan, Korea and Japan to the North and East would be greatly increased."

President Johnson, in his memoirs, wrote:

"If we ran out on Southeast Asia I could see trouble ahead in every part of the globe—not just in Asia but in the Middle East and in Europe, in Africa and in Latin America. I was convinced that our retreat from this challenge would open the path to World War III."

This seems a hoary litany over twenty-five years later, but the history of Indochina since 1975 has demonstrated that it was not a completely erroneous concept. Most important, it was believed at the policy levels of the American government.

This broad thesis, as well as many corollaries, however, were debated only sporadically, not until well after the initial commitments under the basic policy. Most of the internal debate within the government—and it was intense—was over how to apply the policy. The dissenters (except for George Ball, then undersecretary of state) confined their disagreements to the effectiveness that could be expected from given programs. CIA director John McCone's well-known memorandum of dissent of April 1965 (quoted in Lyndon Johnson's memoirs) was mainly a plea for a stronger bombing campaign; he wanted to "hit them harder, more frequently, and inflict greater damage." His point was that given a commitment of ground forces to combat, a constrained bombing campaign would be inconsistent and would probably doom the entire mission. Good advice, but not a challenge to the basic engagement.

It is argued that Johnson's advisers had agreed to only a limited deployment of troops and then became trapped into increasingly larger increments, until of course total American troop levels reached over half a million. This is not very convincing, because there were innumerable stopping points. And one of the major defects of the entire strategy was its ambivalence. Contrary to the popular image in the 1960s of bloodthirsty cold warriors, the Johnson team was tormented by second thoughts. The president and his key aides clearly preferred to negotiate an end to the war, and promoting negotiations became an obsession. But genuine negotiations gradually became more and more unlikely, first because the governments in Saigon were too weak to stand the strain and uncertainties of talks that might end their existence. Later a negotiated settlement came to require some basic North Vietnamese concessions. The one thing that is clear in retrospect is that Hanoi was never truly interested in ending the war short of fulfilling its only real objective—the conquest of all of Vietnam.

Thus the United States found itself in a classic dilemma—forced to choose between winning the war by escalating to a level of risks that threatened Chinese intervention, or securing peace by concessions that would jeopardize South Vietnamese independence, the very object of the war. The dilemma was never satisfactorily resolved.

Ten years earlier the United States under President Eisenhower had refused to enter the war for Indochina that the French were fighting against the Vietminh. Despite some hesitation and debate, the Eisenhower decision, however, reflected the slogan "No more Koreas." America did not want to fight wars on the landmass of Asia, and the Eisenhower administration wanted no part of another limited war.

Why, ten years later, did the United States decide to fight on the mainland and to fight another limited war? In 1954, Eisenhower had strong public support for his decision to stay out of the war in Indochina. But ten years later, Lyndon Johnson, occupying the same White House, had the near-unanimous vote of the Senate to proceed along a course of increasing intervention that seemed to violate Eisenhower's Great Commandment. The *Pentagon Paper*'s editor noted in a summary:

> The landing of the Marines at Da Nang was a watershed event in the history of the U.S. involvement in Vietnam. It represented a major decision made without much fanfare—and without much planning. Whereas the decision to begin bombing North Vietnam was the product of a year's discussion, debate and a lot of paper, and whereas the consideration of pacification policies reached Talmudic proportions over the years, this decision created less than a ripple. A mighty commandment of U.S. foreign policy—thou shall not engage in an Asian land war—had been breached.

There were major differences between 1954 and 1964. The French war was the death rattle of colonialism. The French were trying to preserve an outpost that they had lost during World War II. Until 1950, the United States had viewed the French enterprise with considerable skepticism. Truman shared the typical Midwestern American's aversion to anything that smacked of colonialism, and Washington had doubts about all colonial wars. To some extent these ingrained reactions were tempered by a strong anticommunism, and this created some sympathy for the French. Moreover, no one had a clear idea how to deal with the obvious consequences if the communists should be the victors. At one point George Marshall, then secretary of state, confessed that while he feared control by the Kremlin, he "frankly had no solutions."

By 1952–53, attitudes were changing. In the wake of the Chinese communist victory on the mainland and the Korean War, the United States was beginning to consider intervention to salvage the French. One condition set by John Foster Dulles was that France agree to early independence for the "associated states"—Laos, Cambodia, and Vietnam. At first the French balked at this condition, and Paris feared that American help and intervention might mean a war with China. But then in desperation France asked for help.

The United States debated intervention for almost six months, from late 1953 until the fall of the fortress at Dien Bien Phu. There were hawks who urged various forms of military intervention, from the use of ground forces to an air strike with atomic weapons. Early in this debate Eisenhower insisted that the United States would not go it alone. He wanted allies, particularly the British.

London, however, under the strong hand of Winston Churchill, saw the issues quite differently. Churchill had once quipped that he had lived his life without bothering about these small states in Indochina, and he proposed to leave them alone, if they left him alone. More seriously, he warned Washington against fighting on the "fringes" where the Russians were strong and could mobilize nationalist sentiment. His course was "conversations" at the center, i.e., with the new Soviet leaders. Eisenhower needed no warning about the futility of fighting Russia around its periphery, but he was frustrated by the thought of another loss to the communist conspiracy. Thus he changed his position and was not averse to considering intervention, even if alone: his only unalterable condition was that no ground troops be sent. This left only air power. In the end no help was sent to relieve Dien Bien Phu, and this left negotiations as the only course.

Surprisingly, the negotiated outcome in Geneva in July 1954 was more favorable than anticipated. Of course, Vietnam was partitioned into two states, but divided along the 17th parallel—at Molotov's suggestion. Laos and Cambodia were officially neutral, and a government in South Vietnam under Ngo Dinh Diem was recognized by the conference (Chou En-lai even suggested diplomatic relations). The settlement was imposed by the great powers, Britain and the United States on the one hand and Russia and China on the other. Each had other interests to serve. It is now clear that the Chinese, contrary to almost all opinion in the West, had no desire to see the strengthening of the Vietnamese, their ancient enemy. The Soviets had priority aims in Europe: they saved face for the French government of Mendès-France, and he saw to it that the European Defense Community was killed in the French Parliament. The French were re-

THE COLD WAR IS OVER

lieved to be out of Indochina, and America grudgingly accepted the compromise. As a consequence of Great Power bargaining, the settlement was bitterly resented by the North Vietnamese, and thus the seeds were sown for the resumption of the war. By the next round, in the 1960s, Ho Chi Minh and his comrades would have ended their subservience to their Great Power allies and could exploit the split between Russia and China.

The new status quo in Southeast Asia could have been tolerable for the United States, but Dulles made a fatal error. He eagerly sought to substitute American tutelage for the departing French. The new government in Saigon of Ngo Dinh Diem was taken under the wing of the United States. Security assistance, military equipment, American advisers, and all the trappings of an alliance began to take shape. The outcome of the first Indochinese war was to put the United States in the position of guaranteeing a new ally, if and when the war for Indochina should resume, which the settlement of 1954 unfortunately invited. This assumption of new responsibilities came about with no great public dissent but also without any grand strategy.

━━━

One strange myth dominated this phase: namely, that Indochina was in the Chinese sphere, and that whatever happened there was ultimately the result of Chinese policy. The idea of an "Asian Tito" in Hanoi was occasionally contemplated in policy circles but usually dismissed. Since Washington had no contact with Peking, it substituted Russia for China and sought to talk to the North Vietnamese indirectly through the Kremlin. In a broad strategic sense this was an accurate reflection of the power realities of 1954–55, but by the 1960s Moscow had less and less incentive to take an active role in making peace in Southeast Asia at the expense of Ho Chi Minh, who was a potentially important ally in Moscow's struggle with Mao for the leadership of international communism.

Nevertheless, Washington's reliance on Moscow to exert influence over Hanoi was probably still a valid strategy while Khrushchev was in power.

But after he had been overthrown in October 1964, it was a dubious bet for Washington to make. Moreover, the Chinese had already embarked on a strategy that made it more and more imperative for Moscow to support Ho Chi Minh.

In 1962–64, the Soviets had come under a long vicious attack from the Chinese. An eleven-part series of articles was published attacking every aspect of Soviet internal and external policy. "On Khrushchev's Phony Communism" was a typical title. And beyond these polemics, the Chinese set out to split the various communist parties into pro-Chinese and pro-Soviet factions, and to some extent they began to succeed. This made the support of the major communist parties, especially those in power, even more important for Moscow.

The Chinese also fashioned a new strategic doctrine to the effect that the countryside would overwhelm the cities. This was well tailored for the Asian-African parties. The vehicle for the countryside to conquer the cities was "people's war" as elaborated by Marshal Lin Piao, then believed to be Mao's probable heir. A protracted guerrilla war was an especially appealing doctrine for the North Vietnamese, who appropriated it and espoused it under General Giap's name. Moreover, Hanoi was disenchanted with Khrushchev's apparent détente with Washington; and to make matters worse, Moscow countered the Chinese by proposing a different approach altogether—namely, for local communists to join radicals to create "national democracies," a hybrid coalition that would lead to "socialism" by peaceful means. These new regimes, of course, would cooperate with the Soviet Union, which would safeguard the interests of the local communists. Naturally, the North Vietnamese wanted no part of this.

It is impossible to guess how the intra-communist struggle would have unfolded had Khrushchev remained in power. He had been seriously weakened by the Cuban crisis, however, and was overthrown in a palace coup in October 1964. The coup grew out of the growing chaos in internal policy—Khrushchev's split of the party into two divisions, industrial and agricultural. It may be that the worsening of relations inside the communist movement also played a role in his downfall. In any case, Chou En-lai was invited to the celebrations of the October Revolution in 1964 and traveled to Moscow to meet with the new leaders, who, of course, had been Khrushchev's chief lieutenants and thus not new to the Sino-Soviet conflict. Marshal Malinovsky supposedly insulted Chou by saying, "Now it's your turn to get rid of Mao." Nothing was achieved in Chou's meetings, and the clash continued and worsened. The Chinese were soon denouncing the "hobgoblins" who were praying for Khrushchev's resurrection.

The Vietnamese were immediately sensitive to the change in Moscow. They moved away from the Chinese and toward the new Soviet leaders just enough to justify a trip to Hanoi in February 1965 by the new Soviet premier, Alexei Kosygin. He was in Hanoi when the United States launched its first bombing mission as a reprisal for a Vietcong attack on an American base camp in Pleiku in the South Vietnamese highlands. When Kosygin departed, the communiqué signaled Moscow's willingness to strengthen the "defense capacity" of the North Vietnamese. Khrushchev had gradually disengaged from Indochina, but his successors were in the process of undertaking a new commitment. To be sure, at first Moscow was careful to distinguish between the defense of a socialist state in the north and the war in the south. But this soon became a distinction without a difference.

The Chinese leaders countered by pressing for an even more belligerent line in Indochina. Whatever their previous reservations about the increase in Vietnam's position in the area, by 1965 the Chinese were competing with Moscow for influence in the Vietnamese capital. Chinese motives were fairly obvious: they wanted to undermine any Soviet détente with Washington, to discredit the Soviets among other communist parties, and, above all, to justify an extremist radical position inside China, as a prelude to the revolutionary upheaval of the Cultural Revolution that was soon to break out in Peking. The Chinese therefore accused the Russians of appeasing Washington. They claimed that Kosygin during his stopover in Peking, on his way back from Hanoi, had indicated to the Chinese that he wanted to find a way out for the United States. The Soviets, in turn, implied that Mao had said to Kosygin that Sino-Soviet unity could be restored only by a war with the United States. And the Chinese foreign minister, Marshal Chen Yi, had said that "only by concrete action against U.S. imperialism and its followers can the Sino-Soviet alliance be tested and tempered. . . ."

This was the atmosphere that led to the final decision that American troops would enter the war as combat forces. For Washington, Vietnam seemed to be more and more of a test case for the radical doctrines of the Chinese and General Giap. If "people's war" succeeded, not only would the famous dominoes of Southeast Asia be in danger, but the contagion might spread through the third world.

None of the decisions was put in this crude fashion, but this was the essence of the policy—to contain communism, and especially its more virulent forms in Asia.

Until late 1967 the policy succeeded. Because of subsequent events, this early success is scarcely ever recognized. American forces won all of their battles. The Vietcong and North Vietnamese forces suffered heavy losses, gradually lost the initiative, and were being hard pressed on almost every front. Without the sanctuaries of Laos and Cambodia it is likely that the communists would have been defeated by late 1967. But the Johnson administration could never overcome its strange reluctance to attack these sanctuaries. And as American opinion turned against a prolonged war, there was strong resistance to any escalation of the fighting beyond the borders of South Vietnam; indeed, the pressures were to stop the air war against North Vietnam.

Adverse public opinion in the United States became a strong weapon for Hanoi. It is usually argued that opinion turned against the war because its most grisly features were witnessed on television. More important was the fundamental ambiguity over its purpose. The Johnson administration could never rally latent public support. Nixon's "silent majority" would not demonstrate and sacrifice for a stalemate. Nor could Lyndon Johnson "hunker down," as he put it; he had to tinker constantly with offers of peace, with cease-fires, bombing halts, and innumerable private overtures for negotiations. (This may be a malady of strong presidents.) The volume of documents of the *Pentagon Papers* pertaining to the various negotiating channels to Hanoi, often through private intermediaries as well as the more official channels, makes an appalling record of mixed messages and signals. Little wonder that the North Vietnamese were doubtful that the United States would "stay the course."

Nevertheless, the communist strategists in Hanoi could not afford to gamble on American inconstancy. They decided on a gamble of their own making: to launch a surprise attack during the Tet holidays in January/ February 1968. Violating all of the traditional doctrines of a protracted guerrilla war, the Vietcong guerrillas came out into the open and attacked most of the major cities and urban areas in large organized units. They were slaughtered, in numbers so overwhelming that Washington could not believe the reports from the field in Vietnam.

The Tet offensive, however, was a devastating political blow to Washington. Subsequent studies have exposed the role of the American media in converting a military debacle into a psychological victory for Hanoi. The fact was that the bulk of the Vietcong forces had been destroyed, and only the organized North Vietnamese regular army units remained in the field—to be sure, a formidable force. But the war was no longer a guerrilla war of liberation. It had become a conventional battle between two large armies.

In Washington, however, this was never quite appreciated. The "Wise Men" who counseled President Johnson concluded that the war was over. We will never know what the outcome might have been had the president ordered General William C. Westmoreland to take the offensive against a force that was badly damaged and demoralized. That Johnson took the opposite course is still puzzling; it ran against his entire career and character. Moreover, it was a strategic blunder: virtually to resign in March 1968 and devote ten months to negotiations guaranteed a respite for Hanoi and a dead end for any talks, which did in fact begin in Paris. Hanoi had no incentive to settle with a lame duck that might or might not deliver. The communists reasoned that a new American administration, after Johnson's declaration of failure, would have to make peace. (This calculation reckoned without Richard Nixon, of course.)

=====

Once again the situation was neither war nor peace. But one thing had changed. Johnson was now free to deal with the Soviet Union. For several years, despite the war the administration had tried to enlarge the Kennedy opening achieved by the test ban treaty of 1963; there were periodic contacts and negotiations concentrated on a new treaty to stop the spread of nuclear weapons. There was a strange conjunction of events: on the day that the negotiations opened for this new nonproliferation treaty, Johnson announced a new major increase of American troops in Vietnam. Rusk warned of this potential conflict, but the two superpowers seemed to want to hold on to some slender thread of relations as the situation worsened in Asia. Johnson moved slightly forward in that direction in the bizarre summit meeting in Glassboro, New Jersey, with Premier Kosygin, who had refused to travel to Washington from a UN meeting in New York (June 1967). That brief conversation in Glassboro did not concentrate on Vietnam but foreshadowed the next phase of East–West relations—the competition over strategic armaments. It was the first small step toward the agreement limiting strategic arms that Johnson's successor would conclude in 1972.

But first there was a strange interlude. After several years of fitful negotiations, the two powers along with other countries in July 1968 did finally sign a second arms control treaty prohibiting the proliferation of nuclear weapons (the NPT). This breakthrough, which came after Johnson's speech withdrawing from the presidential race, later led to a private agreement to hold a full-fledged Soviet-American summit meeting. In anticipation of that meeting, Washington developed a proposal to limit strategic arms; it was approved by Johnson in early August 1968 (the proposal was, incidentally, close to that finally agreed on in 1972 under

Nixon). The summit was to be held in the first ten days of October, in the USSR (probably in Moscow), and the public announcement was scheduled for August 21, 1968. On the evening before, however, the Soviet ambassador, Anatoly Dobrynin, informed the president that Soviet units were invading Czechoslovakia. It was "like throwing a dead fish in the face of the president," Rusk later complained to Dobrynin. The summit announcement was canceled, but the idea for a Johnson summit was revived even after the presidential election.

There was a genuine irony in this sudden turn in Czechoslovakia. The collapse of international communism in the 1960s had made it possible for Hanoi to play Moscow against Peking, and thus to thwart Johnson's war. Now that same phenomenon made it possible for the Czech communist party, under the reformer Alexander Dubček, to slip out from under Soviet hegemony in the famous reform program of the "Prague Spring." But not for long. On August 20 the invasion began. The entire Czech leadership was carried off to Moscow; most were purged, and replaced by Brezhnevite stooges, who reigned until the revolution of 1989 destroyed their regime, forced Moscow to denounce the invasion, and brought Dubček back to a position of prominence.

In 1968, however, the old cold war rules still seemed to hold. The West did virtually nothing in retaliation for the invasion, beyond a brief freeze in diplomatic contacts. As Johnson put it in his memoirs, "We could only watch and worry."

American passivity gave rise to one of the more insidious rumors of the cold war: that the United States and the Soviet Union had made a bargain—Washington would have a free hand in Vietnam and in turn Moscow would have a free hand in Czechoslovakia. It was repeatedly and vehemently denied but had a long life, if only because it seemed plausible. According to some Czech officials, such a bargain with Washington was even claimed by Brezhnev in his post-invasion confrontation with Dubček in Moscow. There is no evidence whatsoever for this interpretation, yet this was roughly the outcome. The two superpowers had reinstated the cold war rules of spheres of influence that had been so brutally trampled by Khrushchev in Cuba.

There was an ominous aftermath to the invasion. In September, Moscow declared a new doctrine to the effect that the Soviet Union would be the final arbiter of whether a country was jeopardizing the gains of "socialism." If the Soviet Union decided that such gains were threatened, then Moscow reserved the right to intervene to protect socialism. This was the Brezhnev doctrine, born in an article in *Pravda* on September 21, 1968. Nowhere was this ominous doctrine considered more apprehensively than in Peking. Without knowing it, the Nixon breakthrough to China had been born, and it would finally lead to the end of the war in Vietnam.

———

The Vietnam War had to be fought. The entire thrust of American foreign policy pointed in this direction. To have walked away from South Vietnam while North Vietnamese units overran Saigon in 1965 would have been unthinkable for the men charged with the conduct of policy. Within hours of taking office, Lyndon Johnson exclaimed, "I will not lose Vietnam." Technically he did not; Saigon fell when Gerald Ford was president. But Johnson lost the war in March 1968, when he announced that he would not stand for reelection as president. It was a great tragedy.

If Johnson had no real choice but to fight, he did have a choice in how to fight. This is the great mystery of Vietnam: why the war was conducted in such an erratic way. Partly it was because Johnson was badly served by his advisers. No president should be forced to make tactical military decisions, whether to bomb this or that target, whether to add one or two divisions, etc. It was absurd that the president of the United States was reduced to arguing with his critics about the details of the enemy order of battle. Johnson's instincts had warned him of the perils of Vietnam, but his awe of the Kennedy team's strategic expertise betrayed him. He accepted shallow and bad advice on too many key issues. He accepted the facile theory that graduated pressure in Vietnam would work, as it had in the Cuban crisis (advice from the same men who had conducted that crisis). Moreover, he was too frightened by the dangers of a Chinese intervention, so much so that he limited the air war against the North and the expansion of the ground war into Laos, Cambodia, or even North Vietnam. As a New Deal Democrat he wanted to believe that the social revolution and nation-building he was encouraging in South Vietnam would create a new sense of national purpose and would thus win the war. The concept was sound, but it gradually became irrelevant to the real war. His Texas heritage led him to trust the military, but the Pentagon and the American command in Saigon could never decide which war they wanted to fight, or how, precisely, to fight it. In the end they all suffered together. Lyndon Johnson, one of the most effective domestic political leaders, left Washington deeply discredited.

But that is by no means the end of the story. Vietnam remained at the center of the controversy over American policy for at least another decade. Nixon was trapped much as Johnson was. But he was more determined to end the American role. He was not averse to challenging the Cambodian or Laotian sanctuaries, or bombing Hanoi. His exit from Vietnam however, was political, via Peking and Moscow. After the pathetic debacle of the evacuation of the American embassy in Saigon in 1975, history began to exert its claim to decide what had happened. Thus Johnson's domestic program—Medicare, civil rights—long outlasted the bitterness over Vietnam and did more for the well-being of the country than the harm done by Vietnam. The horrors of Cambodia and the Vietnamese boat people revived the question of whether the United States should have persevered to win. Finally, the very men who fought the war reclaimed their dignity and memorialized it in their monument in Washington. For them it was indeed a noble cause.

The Vietnam syndrome had a longer political life. It was responsible for new and sharper limits on American policy, in Angola in 1975 and later in Nicaragua. President Reagan successfully brushed it aside in Grenada by winning quickly, but in effect heeded its dictum in pulling U.S. marines out of Lebanon. But the Vietnam syndrome too has faded. It was scarcely audible when the U.S. Navy sailed into the Persian Gulf, in what threatened to be yet another limited war. Nor was it even an inhibition when President Bush ordered the invasion of Panama in December 1989.

Thus the paradox: Vietnam was in the cold war tradition, but it was also an aberration. It did not interrupt the very gradual thaw in the cold war that began after Khrushchev's defeat in Cuba.

NIXON'S DÉTENTE

hen Lyndon Johnson and Richard Nixon met after the November 1968 elections, the departing president told the incoming president: "The problems at home and abroad are probably greater than any president has ever confronted since the time of Lincoln." Even allowing for Johnson's tendency to hyperbole, and for the fact that the source reporting Johnson's remark was Nixon, there was a basic truth in Johnson's gloomy appraisal.

The country was badly divided—not only by Vietnam but by the social upheaval of what became known simply as "the '60s." Nixon's election was a conservative backlash against the permissiveness, protest, and rebellion of the period and a backlash against a war that could not be won and could not be ended. Richard Nixon had been elected to end the war. Out of this effort would come a truly surprising development—détente with the Soviet Union. It had not been planned that way. But much like Johnson, Nixon had concluded that the escape from Vietnam would have to involve help at least from the Soviets, and perhaps from the Chinese as well.

Nixon inherited more than Vietnam. Johnson had made an effort to continue Kennedy's post-Cuba diplomacy with Moscow. Even the invasion of Czechoslovakia in August 1968 was regarded as more of an interruption than a turning point in relations. Some of America's allies, notably Germany and France, were eager to resume the process of rapprochement with Moscow after a suitable interval. Moreover, Johnson had a Soviet commitment to begin negotiations on limiting strategic armaments.

Since the Cuban crisis Moscow had embarked on a sustained buildup of strategic weapons. The increase in Soviet strategic weapons was a new factor that would put further strains on American defenses—especially if the United States was forced to build a defense against ballistic missiles, an ABM system. Moscow had a crude system, but many in Washington thought a U.S. system would be far too expensive, and probably would not work. Nevertheless, the Johnson administration had drawn up plans for an ABM, but support in the Congress for the program had begun to sour by 1969. Nixon had to decide quickly whether to pursue the program, which had potentially serious strategic implications if both sides were to engage in a competition for major strategic defensive systems. Moreover, there were growing public and Congressional pressures to open negotiations with Moscow to limit all strategic armaments, both offensive and defensive (the SALT talks).

Obviously, the new administration needed a strategy to deal with Vietnam as well as to wend its way through the various cold war issues.

Neither Kissinger nor Nixon was an ideologue. For them, the battle in Indochina was not only about containing communism, though neither would have quarreled with that objective. Both had been skeptical of containment as too passive. But in 1969 they saw even that minimalist position threatened by Soviet expansion while the United States remained bogged down in Southeast Asia. Moreover, both were conservatives who wanted a strong defense posture; the American strategic arsenal of the 1970s and 1980s was created during Nixon's presidency. Defense was the prerequisite for restoring the balance of power that had been jeopardized by the rise of Soviet strategic power and the decline of the United States during the Vietnam War. They also believed that the Soviet Union could be dealt with, but only from a position of strength combined with a realistic diplomacy that took into account legitimate Soviet interests, especially in Europe (reviving the balance in Europe is one reason why Nixon was the first president to visit a communist country—Romania in 1969). Both suspected that the era of American predominance was probably over, and the United States had to prepare for difficult domestic debates about the purposes of American power, and for an era in which strategic maneuver was as important as a rigid anticommunism.

Above all, they were students and practitioners of power politics, and that led both to China and to the revolution in foreign policy that breakthrough entailed. It is often said that only Nixon, the great anticommunist, could have achieved the China breakthrough. Probably that is true, but it is also true that only Nixon and Kissinger could have conceived of the "China card" and the way it was played in the early 1970s. For both men the opening to China was a step on the road to the real center of power—Moscow. That was where the Vietnam War might be terminated, and it was also where the long postwar confrontation might be ameliorated, if not settled. The end of the cold war in 1989 had its roots in the Kissinger-Nixon strategy twenty years earlier.

In 1969, Vietnam had to be the first priority. Nixon soon ruled out the possibility of winning through a new military campaign. Even with very heavy bombing of North Vietnam, for such a military campaign to be decisive would require months, and the mood of the country was too volatile for another period of turmoil. On the other hand, no conservative Republican administration was going to come into office only to surrender Vietnam to the communists. Therefore a middle option was adopted: to continue the war, to turn over more and more responsibilities to the Vietnamese forces, and to withdraw almost all American troops. Meanwhile, Nixon was willing to bear the political repercussions of escalation by extending the war, briefly, into Cambodia, and later into Laos—also briefly. Finally, the administration tried to draw the sting of its critics by adopting much of the negotiating position the critics had demanded of Johnson (e.g., coalition governments). It proved futile; the opposition at home continued to grow, and the North Vietnamese were intransigent.

If the war was to end, new strategic factors would have to be brought to bear—and the strategic issue that seemed most fruitful was relations with the Soviet Union.

Yet even a new administration in Washington could not simply pick up contacts with Moscow where they had evolved before the invasion of Czechoslovakia. Moreover, Nixon confronted new strategic circumstances. The Soviet Union had improved its power position greatly since the Cuban crisis had forced it to retreat so ignominiously.

In 1969 the Soviet Union claimed strategic equality with the United States, and many analysts in Washington thought Moscow aimed at achieving a strategic superiority. Moscow wanted a ratification of that parity in nuclear weapons, and it still wanted what had eluded Stalin and Khrushchev—American recognition of the legitimacy of the Soviet empire in Europe. Washington, in turn, wanted an arms control agreement that would lead to a more stable strategic balance, not simply ratifying parity. It wanted some greater Soviet restraint in its foreign adventures. Most immediately it wanted help in extricating the United States from Vietnam. In return it could promise only some economic assistance.

In any other circumstances, the Soviet Union would have had no incentive to help the United States out of its Vietnamese quagmire. But two new facts of international life gave Nixon some leverage. First was the increasingly bitter dispute between Moscow and Peking that had erupted in fighting along the Ussuri River in March 1969. Second was the arrival in late 1969 of a new West German government, led for the first time since the 1920s by the Social Democratic party. The new German chancellor, Willy Brandt, was determined to do something about the German national question, even at the expense of Bonn's policy of isolating East Germany.

These new factors led eventually to the three most enduring achievements of the period known as "détente":

(1) This period witnessed the first strategic breakthrough in cold war alignments—the reversal of alliances that occurred in 1971, when Washington succeeded in opening the door to China.

(2) A new and less rigid European security relationship arose out of a limited agreement concerning Berlin (September 1971) and the development of Brandt's *Ostpolitik*. The result was a surprising new relationship between West Germany and the USSR, embodied in a treaty of August 1970, based on a formal West German acceptance and recognition of the division of Germany. Finally, the European Security Conference was convened in Helsinki (July 1975) and concluded agreements that were equivalent to the peace treaty ending World War II.

(3) The SALT agreements of May 1972 (and June 1979) limited strategic offensive arms as well as strategic defenses (ABM); the two deeply hostile superpowers agreed to restrict the very armaments they ultimately depended on for their basic security—a fundamental bargain that has lasted for almost twenty years.

———

The steady worsening of relations between the Soviets and the Chinese in the 1960s was partially obscured by their grudging cooperation in supporting North Vietnam. Soviet military supplies to Hanoi were transported and even airlifted through China. Occasionally the shipments were harassed, but in the main the supplies went through. There were even some in the West who concluded that the dispute between the communist superpowers was only a dispute over tactics. Even at high levels in Washington there was skepticism that the conflict over aging ideological principles had much operational relevance for the United States. After the open military clashes over the Damansky Islands in the Ussuri River in March 1969, Kissinger and Nixon began to consider more seriously whether there might be a chance to improve relations with Peking. At one point in the summer of 1969 the Sino-Soviet border tensions were so high that it even seemed possible that there might be a war between the two communist powers. What had begun as a struggle over ideology and the politics of international communism had degenerated into a traditional clash of two antagonistic powers.

Washington even went so far as to "tilt" toward China; it issued some warnings against any Soviet adventure, such as a surprise military strike against China. Some critics thought that this was mere posturing, but Washington's attitude was carefully noted in Peking. Soon some progress was being made in bilateral contacts, though they were sidetracked for a time by the Cambodian "incursion." Gradually Washington and Peking came to see that their interests coincided: neither wanted to see the Soviet Union establish its hegemony either in the Far East or in Europe.

Meanwhile, Brezhnev was fed up with polemical debates with China. A year after proclaiming his doctrine asserting Moscow's universal right of intervention in the "socialist" world, he began a major buildup of military power along the Sino-Soviet border that reached a force of over fifty divisions within a few years. These were ominous circumstances for China, and the United States loomed as an increasingly attractive counterweight to Moscow's pressures. Only Mao Tse-tung had the power and prestige to engineer a radical and dramatic switch in alignment, and that is exactly what happened. Nixon was invited to send an emissary to China; this led to Henry Kissinger's secret trip of July 1971, which in turn led to President Nixon's formal visit of February 1972.

It was a bizarre spectacle. Richard Nixon, one of the charter members of the China lobby from California, shaking hands with Chou En-lai, whose hand John Foster Dulles had spurned so ostentatiously in 1954; the two old antagonists Nixon and Mao talking amiably in the Forbidden City in Peking; the two delegations drinking toasts in the Great Hall of the People; Nixon visiting the Great Wall and then signing a communiqué in Shanghai that acknowledged there was only one China. One crucial antagonism of the cold war had disappeared.

This diplomatic revolution came about because of the predominance of national interests over ideology—a new characteristic of the cold war that had evolved in the late 1960s. The Chinese were still some years away from the liberal reforms instituted by Deng Xiao-ping. While the Chinese wanted to import American technology, it was a pedestrian consideration for Mao. What he wanted was a new balance of power in Asia to hold off the "polar bear," as he called the Russians. As long as China was threatened from the north, Sino-American relations would prosper—well after Kissinger, Nixon, and Mao had left office. The Soviet threat was also the strategic basis for Jimmy Carter's "normalization" of relations with China in 1979. When the new Soviet leaders who succeeded Brezhnev finally awakened to the gross injury they were suffering as a result of Brezhnev's obsessive fear of China, they moderated their position—and as a result softened the Sino-American alliance. Seventeen years after Nixon's visit, Mikhail Gorbachev arrived in Peking, only to find China on the brink of a popular revolt.

In the 1970s, the American interest was obvious. Immediately after the Kissinger trip, there was the hope that China would influence the Vietnamese to end the war on acceptable terms. And to some extent this happened. The very presence of Nixon in Peking while the war continued was disconcerting to Hanoi (and even more disconcerting was Nixon's summit in Moscow in May 1972 while Haiphong was being bombed).

Neither Nixon nor Kissinger opened the door to China with any illusions that it would produce internal reforms or democracy. Nor were they issues in the Carter agreement of 1979 to normalize relations and exchange formal embassies. The discovery of human rights and democracy as issues between Washington and Peking came a full decade after the establishment of normal relations. In the earlier period of Kissingerian triangular diplomacy, it would have been unheard-of for the United States to apply economic sanctions against a Chinese regime because of the suppression of students in Tiananmen Square. That the relationship could move in this direction in 1989, however, was one more sign that the cold war was waning.

———

The impact on Moscow of the original opening to China of 1971–72 was stronger than Washington realized at the time. The effect was to galvanize the Soviet negotiations with Washington—the talks on both

Berlin and SALT. This was the famous China card, and it worked. It persuaded Brezhnev that détente on Nixon's terms was better than strategic isolation. Thus Nixon was received in Moscow and a SALT treaty was signed, even though the harbor of Haiphong had been bombed.

Brezhnev's morbid preoccupation with China was driven by an elemental racism and a genuine fear that was clear in the private comments he subsequently made to Kissinger. His anti-Chinese strategy was to activate his western policy to secure his flank while he put greater pressures on Peking. In addition, he also tried to draw the United States away from the Chinese through the policy of détente. His western policy coincided with the new West German *Ostpolitik* of Willy Brandt, and this unexpectedly led to a major turn in European politics.

Relations between West Germany and Russia had been temporarily derailed by the Czech invasion. Since 1966, there had been intermittent talks about a treaty banning the use of force. But Bonn was gradually coming to believe that it had to satisfy Moscow's security concerns if any progress was to be made in a rapprochement between the two Germanys. The nonuse-of-force treaty was viewed in Bonn as symbolism. Moscow, however, wanted to go further and extract some recognition for East Germany.

All of this maneuvering was unnerving to Walter Ulbricht, the East German communist leader. And it became more and more worrisome to East Germany as the reforms under Dubček in Prague in 1968 seemed to include carving out a more independent Czech foreign policy toward West Germany. This encouraged some West German leaders who had long thought that there might be a back door to German unification through the conciliation of the Eastern Europeans, thus circumventing Moscow altogether. However, the Polish communist leader Wladyslaw Gomulka supported East Germany's complaints in Moscow. He feared that any agreement between Moscow and Bonn, concluded before Warsaw obtained formal West German recognition of the postwar Polish–East German border (along the Oder and Neisse rivers), would deprive the Poles of critical leverage. As the Czech crisis worsened, the Soviets could not risk the instability of an opening to Germany, and the discussions with

Bonn were broken off. Soviet priorities were clear. In the clash between Brezhnev and Dubček after the invasion, Brezhnev is reported to have screamed that the "results of the Second World War are inviolable, and we will defend them even at the cost of risking a new war."

After the Czech crisis, however, Brezhnev was eager to resume a dialogue with Bonn. He was even more anxious to secure recognition of his Eastern European sphere, including the legitimacy of East Germany. In the new German leader, Willy Brandt, he found a compliant partner. Brandt had given up any hope for clever schemes to outflank the Soviets through Eastern Europe. He adopted a new concept of eastern policy: to draw closer to Moscow and Poland, and then to recognize the other German state. He rationalized this strategy in a shrewd formula that implied ultimate German unification: two states in one nation. Brandt thus overturned a decade of German policy that had been based on isolating East Germany. He signed mutual nonuse-of-force treaties with both Moscow (August 1970) and Warsaw (December 1970) that accepted all of the new postwar borders. And eventually he recognized East Germany in 1972. These agreements inaugurated the era of détente for Europe.

Brandt's diplomacy was running well ahead of his principal ally in Washington. The Nixon administration was wary of Brandt's rapid turnaround in policy, which left Washington to wrestle with the intricacies of a Berlin agreement. Suddenly it had become imperative for the three western powers to sign a Berlin agreement with Moscow, because the West German Bundestag (parliament) had made such an agreement a condition for ratifying Brandt's eastern treaties with Poland and the USSR. The United States could not be more German than the Germans, and the Berlin accords (September 1971) were in fact completed but the Wall remained. The new agreements were based on a Soviet assurance of access to the western sectors of Berlin from West Germany, even though the city would remain divided. Travel for West and East Germans was eased, and after a time East Germany was recognized by the three western powers. There were, indeed, two German states.

This should have satisfied Brezhnev. It was a significant achievement. But Soviet diplomacy is Victorian in its desire for orderly and legal arrangements. Brezhnev wanted his new German package recognizing European borders confirmed in a broader summit meeting, a European Security Conference of all European governments, plus the United States and Canada. The West had resisted this idea since it was first broached by Molotov in 1954. It was regarded as a subterfuge for recognizing the division of Europe. However, the Soviet revival of the proposal for a conference capitalized on the signing of the eastern treaties and the Berlin agreement of 1971–72, and for the first time met with a greater receptivity in Europe. The new agreements created a political momentum toward a European détente, and no western politician wanted to bear the onus for halting the process. The question then became the terms for holding this unwieldy meeting of more than thirty heads of state in Helsinki.

If the Helsinki conference was to symbolize the end of the postwar era, then the West had to know what was to follow. Accordingly, the West insisted on extracting a Soviet commitment to the freer movement of people and ideas as an integral part of détente. In return, Brezhnev wanted what Moscow had always wanted—confirmation of the political and territorial status quo in Europe. He finally achieved this, at least on paper, at the European summit in Helsinki in July 1975. He paid a high price in agreeing to greater human rights in the East. Immediately, dissident elements in the Warsaw Pact countries began to test the outer limits of this new freedom. The origins of Solidarity in Poland owe something to the Helsinki conference (July 1975), as well as the new reform wave in Hungary and the incipient opposition in Czechoslovakia, the Charter 77 group, which included Václav Havel.

The Helsinki agreement was a de facto German peace treaty. The territorial issues and the status of Germany were now agreed throughout Europe. It should have been the end of an era, but it was a beginning, not an ending. What started at Helsinki was to be startlingly different from what Brezhnev expected, the consolidation of the postwar order Moscow had so long desired. Instead, the political status quo in Eastern Europe began to unravel. At first, it was almost imperceptible. Then it gained more momentum until it ignited the Solidarity crisis in Poland in

1979. A decade later, communist rule in that country had collapsed. By Christmas 1989, the old order in Eastern Europe had vanished. Even East Germany—supposedly a bastion of stability—was caught in the upheaval in 1989 when a popular revolt brought down the regime and suddenly the Berlin Wall was irrelevant.

Many in 1975 were harshly critical of President Ford for attending the conference in Helsinki. They had feared the ghost of Yalta. It turned out that the Helsinki meeting was the first step in finally laying that ghost to rest.

The final achievement of this period of détente was the conclusion of the two strategic arms control agreements signed by Nixon in May 1972, and a subsequent agreement concluded by Jimmy Carter in June 1979. The concept for these negotiations grew out of strategic developments in the Johnson era. The idea was simple enough. By the late 1960s both sides had amassed enough long-range missiles and bombers to annihilate each other. There was no need to continue the competition, and an arms control agreement limiting further competition should have been desirable on both sides.

The realities, however, complicated the process. Technology ran ahead of politics. By the time the SALT negotiations were taken seriously (1969), both the Soviet Union and the United States had discovered a new dimension—the possibility of defending against incoming missiles. To be sure, an antiballistic missile system (ABM)—often described as hitting a bullet with a bullet—would be crude and its effectiveness was in doubt. But could either side afford the risk of passing up the opportunity for a genuine defense, even an imperfect one? Suddenly, however, the theorists decided that strategic defense was undesirable and even dangerous.

If one side could defend against incoming missiles, then it might be tempted to launch a first strike, gambling that its defensive system could reduce the weight and damage of the inevitable retaliatory attack. Thus one side might even "win" a nuclear war. Technology, however, was sadistic; it again supplied an answer to this argument. A strategic defense could be overwhelmed and exhausted by launching hundreds or even thousands of missile warheads against it. This meant, however, that each long-range missile would have to be armed with several warheads, which were duly invented and tested, and deployed. This seemed to end the debate over whether to build a defense, but the advent of multiple warheads raised still another horror in the early 1970s.

As missiles became much more accurate, it might become possible for one side to attack the other side's ICBM concrete silos with some assurance of destroying most of them, because multiple warheads allowed an attacker to assign two warheads to each silo, thus greatly increasing the odds of destruction. Requirements for such offensive forces, however, would be in the thousands. This made ICBMs both valuable and vulnerable, and it also meant that missiles on submarines would be at a premium, because, presumably, they could survive at sea and launch a major retaliation. Both sides, of course, wanted large missile submarine forces. And the same was true for heavy, long-range bombers.

The strategic nuclear forces were also mismatched. The United States had a significant lead in multiple warheads and in submarines and bombers, but the USSR had a growing numerical advantage in ICBMs, especially in heavier ones, and in medium-range missiles targeted against Western Europe. Moreover, the Soviet Union had started a small ABM system centered around Moscow and already had a large defense against bombers. The United States had neither, but planned to proceed with its own ABM.

This was becoming a technological and strategic jungle for the politicians. A bargain was not immediately obvious. The two sides had not only quite different forces but clashing military doctrines and operational practices. Nevertheless, in the early 1970s it was becoming more and more obvious that neither side would allow the other to achieve more than a marginal advantage in weapons systems. Both were determined to maintain a rough strategic balance, and that is what made an agreement technically possible.

In the end, however, the technical agreements were signed because of political considerations. Brezhnev wanted to weaken the nascent Sino-American alliance, and Nixon wanted to break out of the geopolitical straitjacket of Vietnam and restore freedom of action to American foreign policy. The agreement was a compromise and a limited one. In effect a ceiling was put on the size of missile forces for five years. More important, both sides agreed in a treaty of indefinite duration to forgo large defenses against missiles. The United States and the Soviet Union were thus indefinitely conceding an unqualified vulnerability to a nuclear attack and trusting in the rationality of the other side. Only the awesome power of nuclear weapons made such an incredible bargain possible between two such bitter opponents. This bargain has lasted since it was signed by Nixon and Brezhnev in May 1972 in Moscow.

Subsequently, more progress on another more permanent offensive agreement was made before Nixon left office, and then under Gerald Ford. This work in defining stricter limits on offensive forces was completed by the Carter administration in a new formal treaty signed in Vienna in June 1979. It was submitted to the Senate, but never ratified. Carter withdrew it from consideration after the Soviet invasion of Afghanistan. Surprisingly, both sides continued to abide by the Carter treaty, which for practical purposes remains in force. The Reagan administration, after campaigning against the treaty, announced it would not "undercut" its provisions. Reagan resumed negotiations with Moscow in June 1982, changing only the name of the talks to START (for strategic arms reduction talks).

The arms race did not end with these agreements. Both sides increased their nuclear arsenals by the thousands. These agreements, however, meant that strategic arms control had become a permanent interest of the two powers, and therefore an element in their relations that would survive the severe changes in the political climate.

The historical significance of the Kissinger years of American foreign policy is relatively clear: he managed the transition from the period dominated by the cold war to a new phase in which elements of the cold war were brought into balance with the new elements of détente, not simply with Russia but with other communist powers. The 1970s brought to a close the era of virulent anticommunism begun in the late 1940s and marked the end of the policy of pure containment.

As détente developed, however, strong anticommunist forces in the United States began to insist on raising the price to the Soviets. For the first time they made changes in the Soviet internal order a condition for better relations. Hitherto, it had been the policy that while the Soviet order was totally unacceptable to the United States, it was unrealistic to expect that changes could be negotiated in Soviet internal affairs. In 1974 the Senate introduced the so-called Jackson amendment (for Senator Henry A. Jackson), tying the free emigration of Soviet citizens, mainly Jews, to the granting of American economic credits or better trade terms to Moscow. The Soviets bitterly resented this linkage and refused to agree. Emigration then dried up. Later, under President Carter, Washington went even further and began to complain about Soviet human rights behavior and express its support for prominent dissidents (e.g., Andrei Sakharov). Again the Soviets were resentful. Nevertheless, the result was that in the 1970s a new issue, human rights, was added to the cold war agenda. It remained there until the reforms of the Gorbachev regime made it less critical. (Ironically, as Jewish emigration revived in the late 1980s, the United States decided to restrict it.)

The new demands on the Soviet Union in the 1970s reflected a deeper public and Congressional disenchantment with détente. Moreover, Nixon was so weakened by Watergate that he was unable to press ahead either with the Soviets or with the American public. A sharp blow was struck by the Middle East war in 1973. Many Americans thought that the Soviet Union should have warned Washington of the impending Egyptian attack across the Suez Canal. For Moscow to have warned Washington, and thereby Israel, after twenty years of investment in the Arabs, would have required far greater incentives than the rudimentary détente of the early 1970s. By 1976, President Ford, faced with this growing backlash, went so far as to abolish the word "détente" from his administration's vocabulary. And while Carter continued the policy in the main, the relationship was eroding.

One reason was that Leonid Brezhnev had less and less to show for his efforts. His aim had been to weaken the Chinese rapprochement with the Americans. He had even offered a secret alliance against China to Nixon, as well as to Ford and Carter. But he failed to tempt them. He went over to the offensive in those soft areas where he could score gains—in Angola, where Cuban troops intervened in the civil war; in Indochina, where the Vietnamese invaded Cambodia after signing a treaty with the USSR; and finally in Afghanistan. Suddenly, it seemed that the worst nightmare of the cold war might be realized—the Soviet Union on the Persian Gulf.

There was a parallel development of equal if not greater importance. A free trade union, called Solidarity, had sprung up in the Gdansk shipyards and demanded recognition, and the Polish communist party was falling apart in the crisis. In 1980, no one could be sure where these startling developments would end. The threat of another Soviet intervention in Poland seemed quite possible.

This was the international backdrop to the American election of 1980. The electorate was dismayed at the turn of events abroad, especially the conjunction of the Iranian hostage crisis and the Afghanistan invasion. This gave Ronald Reagan the opportunity to argue that it was time to rebuild American power and prestige. He got that mandate, and started to fulfill his campaign promises. The cold war was back—or so it seemed. But then Leonid Brezhnev died.

BREZHNEV AND
GORBACHEV

L eonid Brezhnev died on November 10, 1982. For over two years the Soviet leadership was paralyzed. His successor, Yuri Andropov, became ill, and died in February 1984. Konstantin Chernenko replaced him but died a year later. Not until March 1985 did this interregnum end with the Central Committee's election of Mikhail Gorbachev as general secretary, the seventh man to hold the office. A historical turning point had been reached.

More than twenty years earlier, when Brezhnev wrested the party leadership from Nikita Khrushchev in 1964, many American experts confidently predicted (incorrectly) the advent of "Khrushchevism without Khrushchev." When Brezhnev died, no one predicted Brezhnevism without Brezhnev. His legacy was a deepening crisis in almost every aspect of Soviet life, including foreign policy. Nevertheless, few, if any, foresaw the sweep of the Gorbachev revolution that was in the making.

The first step in that revolution was to dismantle the reputation and then the policies of Brezhnev, much as Brezhnev had done to Khrushchev. Yet Gorbachev was to revive Brezhnev's principal accomplishment—the policy of détente with the United States. And he would carry it much further than Brezhnev could have conceived, or would have approved.

Brezhnev's era had been misjudged in the mid-1960s because of the unprecedented nature of his accession to power. No party leader had been overthrown by a coup d'état. Lenin and Stalin had both died in office. It seemed to outsiders that what was involved must have been mainly a preemptive strike to stop further experimentation by Khrushchev. It was not unreasonable to believe, therefore, that the policies of the new team would be a more prudent version of Khrushchev's basic reforms; they were, after all, his protégés.

To be sure, there was an early phase of reform. Within the first year Alexei Kosygin, who had taken Khrushchev's government position as premier, introduced some economic plans that suggested an innovative approach, more solidly grounded than Khrushchev's. The stress was on introducing economic incentives (as opposed to ideological exhortation), reducing the power of the central planners, and giving local enterprises and organizations greater leeway. Industry would be permitted to make a margin of profit, which in turn could be used for investments in the enterprise. Though no one would say so, it appeared that Soviet economists would introduce some elements of a market economy, along the lines of the Yugoslav model.

Of course, there was resistance. Conservatives, who had resisted Khrushchev, were still apprehensive that the role of the party would again be threatened, and that unorthodox economic ideas would infect the political structure. If profits and economic incentives were to be the main guides to production and efficiency, what then of the party's political priorities? Why indeed should the party officials be entrusted with overseeing a complex economic mechanism they no longer understood—compared with the simple task of implementing the production targets set in Moscow?

For a period there had to be compromises. Brezhnev was the chief, to be sure, but the anti-Khrushchev group was more of a collective leadership.

The basic political direction of the new Soviet leadership, however, was indicated in two small steps that would symbolize the Brezhnev era. For most of its history the top policymaking body of the Bolshevik party was called the Politburo, shorthand for political bureau. Under Khrushchev its name had been changed to the Presidium. The top leader had been the general secretary (which had been Stalin's title), the man who presided over the party's secretariat of ten or so officials. But under Khrushchev this too had been changed to first secretary. Within a few months, Brezhnev had changed both titles back to their traditional names: Politburo and general secretary. They were harbingers of a broader decision to soften the de-Stalinization campaign. Stalin would not be rehabilitated, but the periodic assaults against his memory were halted.

It gradually became apparent that the Brezhnev era would be strongly conservative. Khrushchev's "harebrained" scheme to divide the party into industrial and agricultural sections was quickly ended. Party officials who had been the subject of Khrushchevian attacks would be guaranteed virtually lifetime tenure. Their authority would be strengthened and extended into various fields, including not only economics but also cultural policy. Khrushchev had caused Aleksandr Solzhenitsyn to be published, but Brezhnev caused two prominent dissenting writers, Andrei Sinyavsky and Yuli Daniel, to be put on trial.

Gradually Kosygin's economic reforms fell into disfavor or disuse. They were implemented piecemeal and too slowly. Brezhnev clearly was opposed to Kosygin's experiments. His plan was to put new money into agriculture, where he enjoyed some good harvests (because of weather, not planning). And he built housing—at least for a time.

But above all he rebuilt Soviet power. In the Far East against China, the number of Soviet divisions quadrupled. And in strategic weaponry he accelerated Khrushchev's programs, but added the rehabilitation of the nonnuclear forces, including the revival of the Soviet navy. The cost was staggering, and inevitably the funds came out of the civilian economy. To maintain a minimal supply of consumer goods, however, Brezhnev stinted economic investment—one of the more inexplicable decisions of his leadership. But it would be at least a decade before its destructive impact began to be fully appreciated.

The Soviet Union settled down after the turmoil of the decade that had followed Stalin's death. The era of "stagnation," as Gorbachev would call it, was beginning. In the West it seemed quite different, however. Soviet power was in the ascendancy. Brezhnev sought recognition as a true superpower. And he got it at the conference in Helsinki, with all of the European leaders in attendance. He was almost seventy and had achieved more than Khrushchev, and in some respects more than Stalin. The Eastern European empire that Stalin had created seemed guaranteed by the Brezhnev doctrine. Its various leaders had been at the Helsinki conclave, appearing as the equal of the British prime minister, the French president, and the German chancellor. During one of the banquets the East German leader, Erich Honecker, sat next to President Gerald Ford (neither could think of much to say).

Nevertheless, Brezhnev was frustrated. He had not broken the Sino-American alliance; even the death of Mao Tse-tung did not change that strategic alignment, which seemed increasingly to be turned against Moscow. He had received little economic assistance from the West. The United States was still selling him grain, but at high prices, and grudgingly. Economic credits had been cut off by Washington, and the Europeans were not eager to rush in to fill the void. Another SALT agreement was proving elusive, as Ford and Kissinger asked for more and more concessions at the bargaining table but added new weapons, such as the cruise missile, to the American arsenal.

According to Brezhnev, the balance of world power had changed, but the West was stubbornly resisting the implications. Brezhnev was finding it no easier than Khrushchev to translate nuclear power into political gains. And in this mood, an old man embarked on a series of adventures that at first seemed to be a shrewd new strategy but in the end were a disaster. He outflanked the Chinese by underwriting Hanoi's invasion of Cambodia. When the Chinese countered by a small invasion of North Vietnam, however, Brezhnev did not act, even though he would never have a better pretext for confronting China. He then invaded Afghanistan, threatening the Persian Gulf and testing the Sino-American alliance's support of Pakistan. Soviet air bases would soon be within striking distance of the Gulf, and Iran would be virtually encircled—a revolutionary change in the balance of power was under way.

Brezhnev, however, had violated one of the great unwritten rules of the cold war. The Soviet Union could use its military forces with impunity inside its empire, perhaps even against China, but not outside a clear demarcation line, which had been drawn with Stalin in the Iranian crisis of 1946. When Soviet forces for the first time moved outside the empire, the challenge was dramatic and unmistakable, and so was the American reaction.

It is still something of a mystery why Brezhnev sought to conquer Afghanistan, which had followed a pro-Soviet policy since the late 1940s. The immediate cause was the threat to the communist government that the Soviets had helped to install in April 1978, when an internal coup had overthrown the government of Mohammed Daoud. This too was a crude violation of a cold war rule, but the West did nothing, thus contributing in part to the unsettling of Iran, and perhaps convincing Brezhnev that he had been given a free hand.

The Afghanistan invasion was the end of détente. Carter reacted sharply. He withdrew from Senate consideration the SALT treaty he had signed in June 1979 at his summit meeting with Brezhnev in Vienna. He boycotted the Olympics in Moscow and halted the sale of grain. The symbolism was unmistakable: détente had been a bargain of Soviet strategic restraint as embodied in the SALT treaties, in return for American and western economic assistance (i.e., grain sales). Carter ended the bargain. And he would soon also break another cold war rule by beginning to provide aid to the resistance movement inside Afghanistan. No American government, even during the period of Dulles's liberation, had openly opposed the Soviet Union with surrogate forces (Guatemala and the Bay of Pigs were indirect).

It was rumored at the time that Brezhnev had acted in the face of internal opposition—from the KGB (then led by Yuri Andropov, Brezhnev's eventual successor) and from some of his Politburo colleagues. Later, under Gorbachev, the official version from Foreign Minister Shevardnadze was that only a few Politburo members had even been consulted before the invasion. But this version has the virtue of excusing Gorbachev, who by then was a Politburo member. But a military operation of this size could scarcely be kept secret for very long and there were many meetings about it in Moscow that included Gorbachev's patron, Andropov. There was one revelation from the Gorbachev period that confirmed what was widely believed: that Soviet forces participated in the coup that included murder of the Afghanistan president Hafizullah Amin, the man the Kremlin had installed in April 1978.

Some in the West naively thought that Moscow had simply made a mistake that could be repaired by diplomacy. There was an appalling race between Western European statesmen to get to Brezhnev to undo the damage and to assure him that the unpleasantness of Afghanistan need not interfere with détente in Europe. The United States refused to join this stampede, but another more severe crisis was brewing in Poland. Inadvertently, Brezhnev in acting to exploit the opening on his southern flank had exposed the weakness on his western flank and the limits on Moscow's freedom to act with force in both areas simultaneously.

By 1981 Brezhnev had become a pathetic old man, barely able to operate, virtually a caretaker. In the Polish crisis, his apparatus saw it through. Maneuvering to keep some semblance of communist authority in place, the Soviet leadership finally hit upon General Jaruzelski, who imposed martial law in a lightning maneuver that caught everyone off guard in December 1981. It was a clever move, turning the Poles against each other. But it concealed a new reluctance of the Soviet Union to act forcibly against Eastern European dissent. Perhaps a younger, more vigorous Brezhnev would have intervened, as he did in 1968 in Czechoslovakia, but for whatever reason, he refused—or found a less risky alternative in Jaruzelski. Brezhnev, however, had thereby made it almost impossible for his successors to use force when confronted by a far more profound crisis in the summer and fall of 1989, when the communist government collapsed in Poland and throughout Eastern Europe. It was Brezhnev who undermined his own doctrine.

Nevertheless, Brezhnev had bought some time in Poland, but it would be up to his successors to use it wisely in Poland and elsewhere in Eastern Europe. They did not. In dealing with the internal and external crises they inherited, Brezhnev's successors began to experiment with reforms that would jeopardize the very empire Stalin, Khrushchev, and Brezhnev had preserved.

The western reaction to the Polish crackdown in December 1981 was also unusually mild. Nothing much was done when martial law was declared in Poland. True, the Reagan administration adopted some sanctions, but, strangely, they were applied against Poland, while the Soviet Union escaped with a mild reprimand. The arms control negotiations in Vienna proceeded apace, as if Poland were a small, distant country. The West Europeans were even relieved: better Jaruzelski than Brezhnev, they argued. The United States was not ready to go that far, and a split between America and its European allies developed. An era was ending, the era in which on critical East-West issues the Europeans would defer to Washington.

The Europeans wanted to preserve what they could of détente, especially since some of them were under continuing attack for their willingness to support NATO's decision to place American missiles in Western Europe—a replay of the debates of 1957. This time, however, it was not only some Europeans who wanted the Americans out of Europe. For the first time since the debates over Senator Mansfield's periodic resolutions to withdraw American troops from Europe in the late 1960s, prominent Americans began to question whether the Atlantic Alliance was worth it—or whether the United States should act more and more unilaterally, an idea that appealed to the Reagan administration.

In the end wisdom prevailed on both sides of the Atlantic. The Euromissile crisis was managed skillfully. Last-minute desperate ploys from Moscow were rebuffed, and the American missiles began to be installed.

The center in Germany held. There would be a price to pay, later: one of the clever moves to counter Soviet pressures on Germany was a proposal by Ronald Reagan that all intermediate-range missiles should be eliminated on both sides—the "zero option."

It put the ailing Brezhnev on the defensive, and no one in Washington worried that this deadly gambit might be picked up in the endgame by the other side. But an abler, more alert Soviet leadership would perceive the potential for trouble if the backbone of the American nuclear deterrent in Europe was dismantled. To the surprise and consternation of Washington, Mikhail Gorbachev accepted the Reagan offer. It touched off another mini-crisis in the western alliance over the role of nuclear weapons in the defense of Europe.

======

A definitive judgment about the Brezhnev era depends in some measure on the record of his successors.

He made the Soviet Union into a genuine world power. But he did so by risking the long-term well-being of the Soviet state, as his successors were to discover after he died. Russia under Brezhnev had become a military colossus with feet of economic clay. He changed the strategic balance and extended Soviet influence. Gromyko was fond of saying that there was no issue that could be settled without the Soviet Union. In the late 1970s the USSR was in a better global position than in 1964 when Brezhnev seized power. Soviet gains, while real ones, were nevertheless to prove ephemeral in Angola, Ethiopia, and, finally, even in Afghanistan. Moreover, the major power centers—America, Europe, Japan, and China—were aligned against the Soviet Union. Nobody could foresee that the Afghanistan invasion, a strategic coup, would prove to be a "bleeding wound," as Gorbachev would describe it.

Thus the Brezhnev era ended with the Soviet Union besieged on a number of fronts. The final crisis of communism had already begun in Poland, and the crisis of Soviet communism worsened each year.

In the West there was a stubborn refusal to see the true dimensions of the Soviet crisis. The new American administration of Ronald Reagan continued to operate as if the Soviet Union were still on the offensive. Ironically, as it turned out, that was the best posture for the West, even if it rested on an erroneous appraisal of the depths of the new time of troubles in Russia.

14

REAGAN AND GORBACHEV

In Ronald Reagan's first term, Soviet-American relations could not have been much worse. The spirit of those times was aptly summed up by both leaders. President Reagan had proclaimed that the Soviet empire was the "focus of evil in the modern world." And Brezhnev's successor, Yuri Andropov, warned against "any illusions about the possible evolution for the better in the policy of the present U.S. administration."

But there were no dangerous confrontations. It was a period of surprising restraint, especially if one considers that U.S. marines were landed twice in Lebanon; there was a war between Iran and Iraq and a war in the Falklands; a KAL 007 airliner was shot down by Soviet air defense, killing an American congressman; and finally, the Soviet delegation walked out of the INF negotiations and the START talks were halted. Not only did these crises not lead to a new showdown, but within two years the arms control negotiations had resumed, and a few months later Ronald Reagan and Mikhail Gorbachev held the first of their four formal summit meetings.

By the end of 1988, when Gorbachev paid a quick visit to New York, where he met one last time with Reagan, who was accompanied by President-elect George Bush, the cold war was over. Reagan and Gorbachev had agreed on an armistice. It remained for Bush and Gorbachev to work out the terms of the final peace settlement.

After some initial hesitation, they began that process in their summit conference at Malta in December 1989. But by then the revolutionary upheaval in Eastern Europe threatened to overwhelm the superpowers. Not surprisingly, each tried to reassure the other that the new order that would emerge from this revolution should unfold peacefully and gradually. The two confrontationists suddenly found themselves sharing a common interest in European stability. Of all their predecessors, perhaps Winston Churchill could have best understood their predicament in shaping the post-cold-war period.

One reason that superpower relations took such a surprising turn in the mid-1980s was the underlying continuity in the Kremlin despite the change in top leaders. The conduct of foreign policy was still in the hands of the men who had helped to create the détente of the early 1970s— Andrei Gromyko, the foreign minister, and Konstantin Chernenko, Brezhnev's closest aide and colleague, who succeeded Andropov on February 10, 1984, as general secretary of the communist party.

Within a few months Gromyko had reconstructed relations with Washington, and by early 1985 that relationship was back in the mainstream. It was an extraordinary accomplishment, achievable only by a man of Gromyko's great tactical adroitness and single-minded skills. Of course, it entailed a strong dose of hypocrisy and some considerable face-saving, but Gromyko had mastered both in his nearly thirty years as foreign minister. He had survived Stalin and patiently endured the political hazards of Khrushchev's confrontations and Brezhnev's détente. Since 1973 he had been a full member of the Politburo. And in mid-1984 he once again was called on to pick up the pieces of a shattered policy.

He faced the wreckage (partly of his own making) that had been created by the failure to defeat the Americans in the Euromissile confrontations of 1980–84 and the growing consequences of an unwinnable war in Afghanistan. Above all, Gromyko had to reckon with the fact that American power was rising under Ronald Reagan. Classical anticommunism had returned to Washington not only in official rhetoric, but also in military programs and in the reassertion of self-confidence. The hesitation and doubts of the last year of Jimmy Carter had disappeared. Moreover, confrontation over the missiles in Europe was self-defeating, and to continue it would be dangerous for Moscow. The alternative was to revive détente.

The road back for Gromyko was clearly marked. The arms control negotiations had to be reinstated. They were the symbol of détente. The problem was that Reagan had created a nearly insurmountable obstacle by introducing in March 1983 the idea of a perfect defense, the Star Wars plan to defend America from space-based weapons, using exotic new technology. While some American scientists ridiculed it, Soviet strategists had to take it seriously. Andropov had immediately denounced it as a plot to "disarm" the Soviet Union.

It was not a minor issue and could not be circumvented, as many arms control issues had been circumvented in the past. Ronald Reagan would not abandon his new project. He became more and more committed to it. For the Soviet Union to agree to reduce its offensive missiles in the face of the strategic uncertainties of an American space-based defense seemed unthinkable. Gromyko, however, had learned one thing in dealing with the Americans—patience. And he had learned from his previous mentor Molotov that there was always an indirect approach. If Reagan's Star Wars program could not be defeated in an all-out frontal attack, over a longer period it might be reduced to a tolerable level. But this meant that both sides had to get to the negotiating table.

Gromyko tested the waters in mid-1984 with a new proposal to resume talks, including talks about Star Wars. To his obvious surprise, Washington accepted. Both sides were beginning to outsmart themselves, however. Gromyko had not expected an acceptance, and Washington had accepted under conditions it assumed would be turned down. But there was an underlying message. Both sides were groping for a way to restart the engines of diplomacy. Neither wanted to drift further, the Soviets for the obvious reason that their policy was at a dead end, and Reagan because he was entering an election campaign. He had preached negotiating from strength and could proudly claim to have rebuilt that strength. But in 1984 he had to demonstrate that it paid diplomatic dividends. So he had begun to move to the center and to open the door to resume negotiations on arms control. Both sides proceeded gingerly.

By early fall the Soviets had concluded that Reagan would be reelected, and that there was no value in further gamesmanship. Reagan wanted to dramatize his peaceful side, and the result was that Gromyko was invited to the White House in September 1984. Of course, he had been in that mansion many times since he came to Washington as the ambassador in 1943, but never with Ronald Reagan. The meeting therefore had a symbolism well out of proportion to its substantive content. Neither side had yet made any fundamental policy changes, but both wanted the appearance of conciliation. It was agreed that Gromyko and George Shultz would meet again. They did meet in January in Geneva and issued a communiqué that announced in tortured language the resumption of arms control negotiations, with Star Wars on the agenda. The two sides could not even agree on the name for the intended negotiations, lest they compromise their bargaining position. Nevertheless, the impasse had been broken.

This history is important for two reasons. It committed the Soviet Union to better relations with President Reagan well before Mikhail Gorbachev took power. Dusko Doder, the *Washington Post*'s reporter in Moscow, wrote in his book *Shadows and Whispers* that "Chernenko had managed to jettison the confrontational line of his predecessor and restore Brezhnev's old approach toward the United States." And it committed Ronald Reagan in his second term to a course quite different from the one that he was predicting in his first term. Yet this more conciliatory turn was a long way from ending the cold war, and no one at that point would have speculated along such radical lines.

It soon became apparent, however, that the new team in Moscow under Mikhail Gorbachev was not going to settle for business as usual. Radical change was in the air, and it was demonstrated dramatically by the resignation of Gromyko as foreign minister and his replacement by Eduard Shevardnadze, a man without any experience in the field, but with one strong recommendation: he was Gorbachev's man.

A revolution in Soviet foreign policy was beginning. Within four years, the policy so carefully built up by Stalin and his successors was virtually demolished and replaced by the framework for a new policy that made the question "Is the cold war over?" quite relevant.

═══

The revolution in Soviet foreign policy proceeded on two levels—in the operational conduct of policy and in the reconstruction of the policy's doctrinal base.

On the operational level, Gorbachev's policy continued to develop along the lines laid down by Gromyko and Chernenko, moving toward a summit meeting with Reagan and an arms control agreement. The basic reason was the state of the Soviet economy. As more information was revealed, it was apparent that the dimensions of the economic crisis were staggering. Huge budget deficits had been completely concealed; there was sharp inflation, deep corruption, stagnant economic growth, social malaise, and a catastrophic shortage of basic commodities, including food.

Gorbachev desperately needed a breather in foreign affairs to permit concentration on this domestic crisis. The "organic" link between domestic and foreign policy had never been stronger: reform in domestic policy and retrenchment in foreign policy. This is the basic key to the end of the cold war—the exhaustion of the Soviet Union.

Gorbachev recognized that he faced a genuine crisis, but he was uncertain how to confront it. At first he tried to tighten up the system, demanding harder work and greater discipline and attacking corruption, along the lines that Andropov had outlined in his tentative program. But these measures were clearly inadequate, and Gorbachev plunged deeper and deeper into more far-reaching reforms. He was, after all, of a different generation from Andropov's, more open to new ideas, and more keenly aware of the failure of the system. But it gradually became apparent that economic reforms would be sterile without inspiring the population. The principal obstacle, however, was the party bureaucracy, deeply entrenched for eighteen years under Brezhnev and hostile to any innovation. Thus Gorbachev came, reluctantly, to political reform and glasnost. Although he had certainly not planned it that way, he unleashed the centrifugal forces of democracy and nationalism that would begin to tear Stalin's empire apart in Eastern Europe, and inside the Soviet Union.

There is an inexorable logic to political freedom. It cannot be doled out in small doses. In the past, Khrushchev or Brezhnev could turn de-Stalinization on or off, because it was largely an issue confined to the party faithful. But glasnost was something else. As a political necessity Gorbachev was forced to rely on the Soviet intelligentsia against the conservative party cadres. Thus he had to grant some permission to discuss sensitive issues, including the "white spots" in Soviet history (those blank pages covering episodes that had been taboo, e.g., the Hitler-Stalin pact). Inevitably this process mushroomed. Final acknowledgment of the secret protocol in the Hitler-Stalin pact encouraged the Baltic republics to insist on their autonomy, if not independence, on the ground that their incorporation was illegal. The Soviet parliament, in December 1989, refused to denounce the pact as illegal for this reason, and then passed a qualified repudiation.

The unraveling continued and spread to more and more issues and forced more and more political liberalization that was equally devastating. In order to combat the radicals on both the right and the left, Gorbachev decided to build an alternate center of power—the new Supreme Soviet, or parliament, created by limited free elections. The elections proved a sharp rebuke to the party and accelerated the crisis; similar elections were demanded in Eastern Europe. Gorbachev shrewdly put himself at the head of his new institution, but then he found that he had created a true Frankenstein's monster. The new parliament wanted a real voice in policy, and Gorbachev was trapped. Whatever his original design, he found himself conducting a broad revolution that was overturning the system he had inherited from Brezhnev, Khrushchev, and Stalin.

This revolution spread to foreign policy. Gorbachev had to adopt a defensive strategy, which was obscured to some extent by excellent public relations and his own dynamic and engaging personality. He had no choice but to reduce commitments, avoid new ones, and settle for a prolonged strategic stalemate with the United States. He desperately needed to cut his defense spending, but he needed some guarantee that the United States would settle for a stalemate and not press him to the wall at a moment of great weakness. Hence his willingness to make concessions, including conceding to Ronald Reagan in arms control negotiations. He surprised everyone by accepting the Reagan "zero option" to eliminate missiles in Europe. What had begun as a "breather" was evolving into a new foreign policy.

Most indicative of the new policy was the decision to liquidate Brezhnev's adventure in Afghanistan, but without winning the war. Gorbachev had described it as a "bleeding wound," and by 1988 had negotiated the terms for a Soviet withdrawal, in conditions that seemed at the time a certain defeat for Moscow's clients, who would remain in Kabul. (That this did not immediately happen does not take away from the significance of the Soviet decision. Moscow had reason to believe, as did the West, that the puppet regime in Kabul would be routed.)

The invasion of Afghanistan in early 1980 had loomed as an aggressive Soviet thrust in the expansion of Soviet power into the Persian Gulf. After five years it had turned into a defeat. The war was fought within narrow limits, much as the United States had fought in Vietnam. There were limited search-and-destroy operations by Soviet forces into remote mountainous strongholds, followed by complete withdrawal to urban base areas. There may have been a ceiling on troop levels (around 120,000). There was no hot pursuit across boundaries, and no retaliatory raids were made into the sanctuaries of Pakistan or Iran. No real effort was made to stop outside support from the United States and others for the anti-Soviet rebels. Much as Nixon had met Brezhnev when the latter was supplying the Vietcong, Gorbachev met Reagan when Washington was arming the mujahedin.

When Gorbachev insisted on terminating the war without victory, the limits of Soviet power had been demonstrated, much as the limits of American power had been demonstrated in Vietnam. One Soviet official commented that "every other major power has lost a war. . . . Until now that has not happened to us, but now we will be like everyone else."

The chief difference was that Afghanistan was on the Soviet border, and Vietnam was several thousand miles from the continental United States. Vietnam was the end of the affair and the wounds healed. But for the Soviet Union, Afghanistan blended into a general crisis of the entire system.

It was this general crisis that accelerated the deeper revolution in Soviet foreign policy, a revolution that went to the very roots of the Leninist foundations of that policy. A systematic attack on past policy and strategy was conducted by the new minister, Eduard Shevardnadze, and his various academic advisers, but the inspiration was Gorbachev's. It was the new general secretary who said, shortly after taking office, that confrontation with the United States was not an "innate defect in [superpower] relations . . . it's an anomaly." His reappraisal of foreign policy became a vital element in the broad opening of Soviet society—glasnost. Gorbachev seriously challenged long-held propositions about the nature of international relations, the Leninist character of Soviet policy, and the outlook for the longer-term balance of power and thus the very roots of the cold war.

The strong ideological dimensions of Soviet foreign policy were strengthened by the cold war, and in turn sustained it. Marxist-Leninists claim that the foreign policy of any given state reflects its internal social and economic order and international relations are therefore a form of the class struggle. Thus the clash between communism and capitalism was historically inevitable. The cold war could be explained by capitalist resistance to the historical triumph of socialism, which forced continuing confrontations between the two systems. The operational conduct of foreign policy, however, was determined by the balance of forces. Historically the balance had to favor "socialism," but at any given moment the balance was subject to change, and that volatility in turn would determine whether Soviet policy could advance or retreat. In any case, military power was critical in protecting the gains of socialism and the security of the Soviet state from capitalist threats and encroachments.

Because the struggle between capitalist states and communist states was a fundamental clash, it could not be settled simply by agreements. One side was destined to prevail. When and how were open to debate, but they were tactical questions, subordinate to the major thesis of the primacy of the class struggle.

To be sure, these orthodox doctrinal positions were softened after Stalin's death, and Khrushchev introduced the idea of peaceful coexistence as an interim accommodation. It implied that while the struggle would continue it would not inevitably lead to war (this latter modification having been introduced over Mao's violent objection). Nevertheless, the ideological underpinning of a class-oriented foreign policy was never disavowed. It could not be without opening the vast panoply of Soviet ideology, domestic and foreign, to a wholesale revision. Yet this is what happened under Gorbachev.

A "fundamental new philosophy of international problems" was developed, under the slogan "new thinking." By 1988, the class struggle as a basis for Soviet foreign policy had been virtually repudiated. It was the existence of nuclear weapons that made such a massive revision necessary. Soviet ideologues asserted that it would be suicidal for the class struggle between two systems to be resolved by a conflict between nuclear-armed states. If, however, there could be no victory in a nuclear war, then the Prussian strategist Clausewitz was wrong: war could not be a continuation of politics by other means. Preparations to fight a war would have to be balanced with concepts of arms control and deterrence, and both led to more emphasis on mutual security.

But in these conditions, what would be the purpose of Soviet foreign policy? According to Gorbachev's chief ideologist, Vadim Medvedev, peaceful coexistence could no longer be a tactic or a respite, but had to be considered as a "prolonged, long-term process the historical limits of which are difficult to define." Gradually, in place of the class struggle a far more benign idea emerged: that certain universal human values and concerns transcended the class struggle, and the overriding universal concern in the nuclear age had to be self-preservation. The earlier facile notion that capitalism and communism would develop in parallel was declared to be "obsolete"; more likely was that the two systems would intersect.

The new ideology of Soviet foreign policy was summed up by Gorbachev in his book *Perestroika:*

"Ideological differences should not be transferred to the sphere of interstate relations nor should foreign policy be subordinate to them, for ideologies may be poles apart, whereas the interest of survival and prevention of war stand universal and supreme."

For the West all of this seemed a rather archaic debate over worn-out theses from the nineteenth century. But inside the Soviet hierarchy it was explosive. It produced a sharp reaction from orthodox conservatives, who attacked Gorbachev openly for his revisionism. But he prevailed.

Gorbachev prevailed in part because it was clear that an important corollary of Soviet doctrine was not true: the socialist camp was clearly not in the ascendancy. All previous Soviet leaders had claimed that the balance of world forces was moving in favor of the communists, but no one believed that any longer in the 1980s. Supposedly, the communist system was destined to triumph over capitalism because of the inevitable "crisis of capitalism." Clearly that crisis was not at hand, nor was it likely, and Soviet ideologists had to admit it. It was the socialist system that was racked by a crisis of enormous proportions.

In such circumstances the idea of prolonged peaceful coexistence was more and more appealing. But if so, how would Soviet security be preserved? The protection of the Soviet state had rested, after all, on a simple idea—that the USSR had to be stronger than all of its enemies. Thus if the United States moved to increase its military position, the Soviet Union had to overcompensate. This imposed an enormous defense burden that was a strong, perhaps decisive, factor in the crisis in the USSR.

The answer was obvious: the USSR would have to behave like other

Great Powers and rely far more on political means to defend its security. Heretofore, Soviet diplomacy was heavy-handed, befitting its role as a mechanism to deceive, disarm, and dissemble. Now under Gorbachev a policy of extensive maneuver was required. Soviet diplomacy would be assigned the more conventional task of guarding Soviet interests through negotiations, conciliation, coalitions, and even concessions.

All of this would be especially difficult because at the same time, reductions had to be made in Soviet defense to save the civilian economy. Gorbachev made a virtue out of necessity. Reducing the defense burden was transformed into a major doctrinal change. Strategic superiority and "war-winning" capabilities were discarded as defense criteria and replaced by the vague western-sounding doctrine of "reasonable sufficiency" or "defensive defense." The professional military was clearly not pleased with these new formulations, but Gorbachev won. For the first time in decades, if not since 1917, Soviet military spending and Soviet forces began to shrink.

This basic strategic reappraisal indicated that in another important area, the third world, Soviet policy would also have to change. If, for an indefinite period, the USSR would be on the defensive, then it could not afford adventures abroad that might endanger its internal policy priorities. Nor could it afford to take on new clients that would add to the heavy drain on Soviet resources. The Reagan doctrine threatened to make the third world a more dangerous strategic frontier. Retrenchment in this area was called for as well.

Finally, there was a new openness in discussing the history of Soviet foreign policy. For the first time it was admitted, albeit grudgingly, that the Soviet Union had to bear a considerable responsibility for the cold war. One historian even went so far as to assert that the West was justified in regarding the Soviet Union as a dangerous adversary that wanted to eliminate its opponents by military means. Another Soviet writer claimed that "unquestionably" the "severe exacerbation of tensions" in Soviet-western relations in the late 1970s and early 1980s could have been avoided because the tensions were caused by the miscalculations and incompetence of the Brezhnev regime. Such critics went on to argue that in the invasion of Afghanistan, the expansion of Soviet power reached "critical limits"; only the existence of nuclear weapons prevented the situation from unleashing a war. Even Shevardnadze openly admitted the invasion was an error. Such a historical cleansing was a prerequisite for the deeper reexamination of responsibilities for the cold war. No change in basic foreign policy would have been possible without coming to terms with Soviet history.

In sum, Gorbachev significantly altered the ideological foundation of Soviet policy, and on this new base a different superstructure was being erected that was less ideological and more geopolitical. No longer could Soviet policy be rationalized as a temporary respite until the next capitalist assault or the next communist offensive. A more permanent new relationship would have to be built that was secure enough to permit a reduction in the burden of defense. And military means could no longer be the principal pillar of Soviet security. The struggle with the capitalist system would have to end. Mikhail Gorbachev recognized that he would have to come to terms with the United States.

The end of the cold war was coming into view.

═════

None of this Soviet reevaluation was simple, nor did it proceed in a vacuum, developed in some dank library of a Marxist institute. It was worked out as Gorbachev proceeded to anticipate its outcome in his daily conduct of policy. The record is well known. Four summit meetings with Ronald Reagan, including a Kafkaesque encounter in Reykjavik when the two leaders debated the terms for wiping out all ballistic missiles. An arms control agreement in 1987 that did in fact eliminate all intermediate-range missiles. Two visits to the United States by Gorbachev and a return visit by Reagan to the heart of the evil empire, walking around Red Square with Gorbachev.

Partisans of President Reagan argue that his policies brought about the change in Moscow. The Gorbachev revolution was purported to be a vindication of the classic containment policy, because the original concept was that the USSR would begin to change if blocked from external expansion. This goes much too far, but there is no doubt that the strong position adopted by the Reagan administration contributed to the reappraisal of Soviet foreign policy and especially the decision to reach an agreement on eliminating all intermediate-range nuclear missiles—the centerpiece of the Reagan–Gorbachev détente. The deployment to Europe of these missiles capable of reaching Moscow was traumatic for Soviet strategists. It drastically cut their warning time. Such a new instability was all the more alarming if the United States went forward with its Star Wars program. The idea of a quick American strike launched from Europe, backed by a defense against incoming Soviet missiles, revived all of the old fears about the defensive-offensive balance that were laid to rest in the agreements of 1972.

Now the United States was unbalancing that equation by proposing to defend itself. If successful, of course, the United States, protected by an airtight defense, could dictate its terms to a defenseless Soviet Union. On the other hand, if the Soviet Union engaged in the same defensive race, there would be a premium on striking first as soon as it appeared that the other side was on the verge of winning the race to a Star Wars defense. It mattered little that many if not most experts scoffed at the idea of a foolproof defense. Neither side could afford to allow the other to open up a significant lead. This fear explains why Moscow blatantly had already cheated on the ABM treaty by building the large radar at Krasnoyarsk (which Shevardnadze admitted was a treaty violation).

Gorbachev decided to make the ending of the Star Wars program his major objective at the second summit at Reykjavik. But he miscalculated Reagan's obstinacy in defending his favorite project, and the summit collapsed over this issue. This could have been a sharp turn for the worse. No summit had collapsed so dramatically. Yet within a few months the damage had been repaired and the third Reagan–Gorbachev summit saw the signing of the INF treaty banning all intermediate-range missiles, followed by President Reagan's appearance in Moscow.

Clearly there were some fundamental trends at work overriding the tactics of each side. Both were prepared for a new relationship, Gorbachev because of necessity and Reagan because of instinct. In early 1984 Reagan had said that the United States was "in its strongest position in years to establish a constructive and realistic working relationship with the Soviet Union." Few had believed him, but with considerable help from Mikhail Gorbachev, he turned out to be a prophet. His "positions of strength" paid off in arms control agreements.

It is also true, however, that the Reagan administration moved from its original position. This shift was not the sweeping revolution that took place in the USSR, but nevertheless American foreign policy changed considerably. The deep distrust of the Soviet Union gave way to a highly personalized relationship reflecting the apparent friendship between the two leaders—testifying once again to the weight of personalities in politics.

By 1988, President Reagan's initial anticommunism had been replaced by a tribute to the changes in the Kremlin: the president's assessment was that they could no longer mean their Marxist rhetoric if they were prepared to give up some nuclear arms. After his final meeting with Gorbachev, Reagan said:

"Possibly the fundamental change is that in the past, Soviet leaders have openly expressed their acceptance of the Marxian theory of the one world communist state. . . . Their obligation was to expand and make the whole world [communist]. I no longer feel that way."

There were many close to the president who doubted that Mr. Reagan's original harsh rhetoric should have been taken at face value; they said that he was always a pragmatist. Words still count in public affairs, but it was the substance of his original policies—a heavy buildup of military power, the Reagan doctrine of opposing communist regimes and movements, and the insistence that any arms control involve the reduction of Soviet forces—that helped prompt the Kremlin's reappraisals. In the end, however, Mr. Reagan sensed that something different was happening inside the Soviet Union, and he followed the plan of many of his predecessors in moving from the right to the center, from containment to conciliation. Only this time it seemed to work. Thus it was that Ronald Reagan, of all people, helped to end the cold war.

———

In the eight years since the invasion of Afghanistan had wrecked détente, both superpowers had changed. Both had come to realize that there were no real alternatives to some form of coexistence. Neither could defeat the other in a war or in an arms race. Neither could gain a decisive strategic advantage in the third world. Both were overextended at home and abroad, both were declining relative to the rest of the world's great powers. The era of their unquestioned domination of international politics was ending, and the postwar period was coming to a close. It was time to end the cold war—if only out of self-preservation.

15

LAST ACT

There was one final dramatic act to play out before the cold war could be definitively closed out. It was the revolution in Eastern Europe. This is where the cold war had begun, and it was fitting that this is where it would end.

It was the survival of the Soviet Union itself that motivated Gorbachev to undertake his astounding gamble in Eastern Europe. He recognized that once the process of reform took hold inside the USSR, Eastern Europe could not be immunized from its infection. But in Eastern Europe reform was tantamount to revolution, because the regimes there had no roots. They could not reform themselves into legitimate governments; their legitimacy lay in the implied threat of Soviet intervention—the Brezhnev doctrine. Rather than wait to be confronted by a series of potentially dangerous crises that might force Soviet military intervention, Gorbachev in effect wrote off his comrades in Eastern Europe. He could save them only by jeopardizing his own position at home.

It had been an article of faith that the Soviet Union would never countenance the loss of control by the local communist parties, or the abandonment of the Warsaw Pact. To enforce these demands had been the underlying objectives behind the intervention in Hungary in 1956 and Prague in 1968. Both propositions were tested in the summer and fall of 1989. The first disappeared in the Polish crisis in August. Once this barrier was breached, there were some strong doubts over the future of the Warsaw Pact, or at least the role of Soviet troops in Eastern Europe.

For a time, Gorbachev's attitude toward the Brezhnev doctrine was ambiguous. There was some evidence of his attitude when in Czechoslovakia, Husák was pushed out into the presidency in December 1987, and replaced by Miloš Jakeš. More than anyone, Husák had been the symbol of the Soviet invasion. Moscow had also endorsed the removal and denunciation of János Kádár in Hungary and the rehabilitation the memory of Imre Nagy—a strong repudiation of the Hungarian invasion. By mid-1989, Gorbachev was prepared to go further. He began to spell out a repudiation of the Brezhnev doctrine, though couched in broad terms. He told the Council of Europe in July that any attempt to limit the sovereignty of another state would be "inadmissible." The Brezhnev doctrine, of course, had rejected an "abstract, nonclass approach to the question of sovereignty." So there was no mistaking Gorbachev's allusion. And lest there be any misunderstanding, he also said that his concept of a common European home ruled out the threat or use of force between and "within alliances." A few days later the Hungarian foreign minister said that the period of enforcing the Brezhnev doctrine was "over once and for all." There was still skepticism in the West because when one of the hard-liners in Moscow—i.e., the Politburo member Egor Ligachev—justified the invasion of Czechoslovakia. Though he did not invoke the Brezhnev doctrine, Ligachev said that the Czech leadership had "asked for assistance." The implication was that if faced with a similar "request" Moscow might repeat the actions of 1968.

Nevertheless, Gorbachev was moving away from intervention. It was at this time, in the summer of 1989, that Gorbachev and President Bush began their secret dialogue concerning a summit meeting. Moreover, Secretary Baker and Foreign Minister Shevardnadze had apparently talked about the issue of Eastern Europe in July; Baker later said that he had been given assurances against any Soviet intervention.

The critical turning point came in March 1989, when the limited free elections in the Soviet Union established, albeit tentatively, the principle of political pluralism. In Poland in June similar elections were held; they were a resounding repudiation of the communist party. The communists tried but failed to put together a new government. Then Solidarity offered to form a government. The decisive moment came in August 1989, almost fifty years to the day since Poland's death warrant was signed by Hitler and Stalin. In a publicized telephone conversation with the Polish communist leader Mieczyslaw Rakowski, Gorbachev advised him to join the noncommunist government of Tadeusz Mazowiecki. The Brezhnev doctrine was virtually dead.

Gorbachev's advice to the Polish communists was a massive signal that the old guard in Eastern Europe could not count on a Soviet rescue. It reverberated throughout the Warsaw Pact. The Hungarian communists desperately sought survival in the dissolution of their own party, and in the renaming of both the party and the state. The Hungarian Socialist Workers' Party and the Hungarian People's Republic simply disappeared. It was a highly symbolic act, but the Hungarians had been in the vanguard of eastern reform, well before Gorbachev. The attack on the primacy of the old communist party, however, was an important sign of the times—it would eventually spread throughout the east, and to the Soviet Union itself. Of immediate importance, the Hungarians decided to open their borders, causing a crisis with East Germany.

The hard-line conservative holdouts were next: East Germany, Czechoslovakia, Romania, and Bulgaria were the so-called gang of four.

East Germany was supposedly a special case. It seemed inconceivable that the Soviets would permit experimentation on the front line of the cold war confrontation. Moreover, the experts agreed that East Germany had managed to preserve something of the old German national feelings; the traditional bourgeois German virtues—hard work and a respect for authority—could be found in the east, not the west. And during the tense period of the early 1980s, Erich Honecker had tried to preserve a line to his West German counterparts. He even found himself the subject of a debate over his planned visit to West Germany. The Hungarians were urging him on, but the Czechs were attacking it. In the end Moscow intervened and vetoed it, at least for a time. He later did visit West Germany, including his old home in the Saar. Later his spirit of independence was demonstrated again when he became one of the critics of

Gorbachev's perestroika. This proved to be a fatal error. When the crisis came, he had no credit with the Gorbachevites. In the end the regime of Erich Honecker collapsed, after Gorbachev's visit to Berlin proved to be the kiss of death. Soviet troops would remain in their barracks. There would be no German version of the Brezhnev doctrine. During the crisis in Berlin, Moscow passed the word to Washington that there would be no Soviet military action. Honecker was removed on October 18 and succeeded by Egon Krenz, his loyal deputy, who suddenly was supposed to be Germany's Gorbachev. In desperation, Honecker's successors tried to relieve the pressures by opening the Berlin Wall as a safety valve. All that it accomplished was to reveal the total bankruptcy of the regime. Krenz could not last, and he was eventually replaced by Hans Modrow, a party leader from Dresden. Within weeks the Brandenburg Gate would be opened in the presence of the West German chancellor, while the crowds chanted, *"Ein Deutschland."* The dreaded "German question" was suddenly back at the top of the European agenda.

The Czechs were next. The experts made the same predictions, that Czechoslovakia would be a tougher case. But unlike the East Germans, the Czechs had a ready-made opposition and could invoke the tradition of 1968: there was Dubček, more of a symbol than an active force; but there were also the remnants of the Charter 77 Group, and especially the playwright Václav Havel, who had been arrested again in January but became the voice of the revolution (and eventually the new president). The pattern of East Germany—the huge popular demonstrations in Leipzig that brought down the regime—was repeated in Wenceslas Square. The Soviets also took a hand. As the crisis worsened, they warned the Czech leaders against "excessive caution" in pursuing reforms.

Both bastions of communist conservatism suffered the same fate because neither could play the Soviet card, and both shrank from armed force, though it should not be forgotten that in East Germany and Czechoslovakia there were two violent incidents. In Germany it took weeks, but in Czechoslovakia it took days. The successor regime in Prague officially proposed that negotiations begin on the withdrawal of Soviet troops.

Maintaining these garrisons had became difficult for Moscow to justify, when a few days earlier both the Soviet leaders and the others in the Warsaw Pact (minus Ceausescu) had denounced the invasion of 1968 in a formal proclamation, thus depriving the Soviet forces of any legitimate basis for remaining.

These two rebellions also exploded another cold war myth—that the disaffection in communist countries was provoked by poor economic conditions. East Germany and Czechoslovakia were the two most prosperous countries of the Warsaw Pact. What the people wanted—once they realized that the Soviets would not interfere—was, quite simply, freedom.

In far-off Bulgaria, Todor Zhivkov, a shrewd old fox after thirty-five years in power, quickly departed. Here, too, the word was passed from Moscow but Zhivkov was arrested.

This left only Nicolae Ceausescu in Bucharest, trying to withstand the avalanche. The situation in Romania was most instructive in terms of the end of the cold war. Ceausescu had accomplished the miracle of alienating both Moscow and Washington. He had created a bloody-minded personal dictatorship. As the pressure grew, he resorted to a slaughter that dwarfed Tiananmen Square. The vicious fighting was a potent reminder how dangerous the collapse of the Stalinist empire could have been, even though Ceausescu was no longer simply a clone of orthodox communists; he was propped up not by the communist cadres but by the secret security services. It has been revealed that even before the rebellion some opposition leaders may have received Moscow's endorsement to remove Ceausescu—a weird form of Soviet intervention. During the extensive fighting, the opposition National Salvation Front hinted at a request for Soviet intervention; the Soviets were in fact sympathetic, but made it clear in a public statement by the premier that Moscow would under no circumstances take military action. The United States, through the secretary of state, made the remarkable statement that Washington would not object if the Soviet Union did intervene. The French foreign minister was also sympathetic to Soviet intervention, but suggested that a French brigade might be provided as well, though the president of France later said emphatically that no western power should become involved. By Christmas Day, 1989, when Ceausescu was executed, the cold war had been left far behind.

How could this have happened so swiftly and completely? Perhaps the best explanation was provided by Václav Havel, who wrote that "the tide turned and the concept that turned it was the old . . . concept of human rights." Others, especially in the United States, claimed that the revolution came about because the United States and its allies were "determined to stand up more firmly than ever," as the *Wall Street Journal* editorialized. Still others emphasized Gorbachev's refusal to intervene. There is something in all of these points, but there is also another fundamental aspect: the woeful condition of communism in Eastern Europe after forty years.

The system had become thoroughly corrupt. The indigenous communist leadership in most of Eastern Europe had degenerated into a venal, arrogant oligarchy, living like oriental potentates while their own people were desperate. To be sure, Stalin's generation in Eastern Europe (Tito, Dimitrov, Ulbricht, Beirut) were his obedient puppets, but they were also the true believers portrayed by Arthur Koestler in his novel *Darkness at Noon*. By the 1980s, the East European communists had become unprincipled cynics and hypocrites. They believed in little. When the crisis came, they had no moral stamina, and it was easy for one leader to turn against another—e.g., Egon Krenz ordered the arrest of his patron, Erich Honecker. After forty years, almost all of the communist parties could meet in their capitals and vote themselves out of existence without even a whimper. Most realized that in the end their fate would be decided in the Kremlin. It had been an article of faith, however, that Moscow could not afford to sacrifice its satellites, whether they were reformers or hard-liners, inept or efficient, loyal or deviant. Therefore, it would not matter what the people did. This was the most fundamental error, and all of the communist parties of Eastern Europe paid a high price for such an elementary mistake.

It may well be that Gorbachev himself miscalculated. Surely he expected that after the old guard was removed, their successors could stabilize the situation. Stalin would have understood, however, that if the street crowds could bring down one regime, there was no stopping point. But Gorbachev evidently did not appreciate the depth of the disaffection. He was not alone: the first round of successors themselves seemed to share his view. Krenz in Germany, Urbanek and Adamec in Czechoslovkia, Pózsgay in Hungary, Mladenov in Bulgaria, and the various Romanians—all seemed to believe they could survive by uttering reformist slogans, manipulating symbols, changing party names, and shuffling ministries. None of this would satisfy the streets, where the real power was. Thus the upheavals in Eastern Europe followed an inexorable law of revolution: the pendulum continued to swing until virtually all of the old regimes were swept away. Would-be communist reformers went almost as quickly as the diehards.

Not only did the communist system disappear, but any residue of Soviet influence and control was virtually gone as well (expect perhaps in East Germany). The new leaders in Prague, Budapest, and Warsaw all made the same demand: that Soviet forces be withdrawn forthwith. Gorbachev, having abandoned the threat of intervention in the first phase of the revolution, found that it was too late to revive it in the last stages. And even if he had been so disposed, the loss of Eastern Europe began to pale before the threat to the Soviet Union itself—in Lithuania, Moldavia, Azerbaijan, and Central Asia.

The Red Army began to go home. The first contingent left Czechoslovakia on February 26, 1990, as Václav Havel signed an agreement on their withdrawal with Mikhail Gorbachev in the Kremlin. And in a bitter irony, the new Czech government named its new ambassador to the Kremlin: Rudolf Slansky, Jr., the son of the man whom Stalin had purged and executed in 1952.

Once the facade of communism was ripped away, Eastern Europe began to resemble the diverse collection of states that it had been before World War II. Democracy was strongest in Czechoslovakia, where there were genuine roots. The East Germans voted with their feet and at the ballot boxes for unity. The Romanians were floundering, trying to rid themselves of the communist holdovers; and the Bulgarians were having trouble finding politicians to lead the opposition. And the Warsaw Pact was almost an empty shell.

The Poles, however, had second thoughts about severing the Soviet connection as they contemplated the power of a united Germany once again on the Oder-Neisse border that had been dictated by Stalin at the war's end, as compensation for the large chunks of Polish territory he kept. Suddenly this border looked dangerous, and the Poles wanted reassurances, especially since the Western allies had been reluctant to accept this border without a German peace treaty. Roosevelt and Churchill had acquiesced grudgingly, and Churchill had warned against "stuffing the Polish goose" with German territory. But forty-five years later it was Thatcher, Mitterrand, and Bush who felt compelled to insist on the validity of this Polish border, to the visible irritation of their German allies. Stalin would have appreciated this squabbling: after all, he had realized that Poland would have to look to Moscow if Germany ever revived. The cold war was ending, but the old issues were returning: suddenly, what was said at Yalta and Potsdam in 1945 was as important as what was agreed at Helsinki in 1975.

Another ghost of World War II reappeared in Ottawa, Canada, on February 14, 1990: the foreign ministers of the old wartime coalition—Britain, France, the United States, and the Soviet Union—announced that henceforth the German question would be considered by the two German states plus the four powers—the so-called "two plus four" formula. It is worth noting that Britain, France, and the Soviet Union would have preferred "zero plus four," the old Yalta and Potsdam formulas, excluding the Germans altogether. Only the United States held out for the Germans. No American government would be caught in a replay of Yalta.

But the post–cold-war issues of 1990 that confronted the new leaders of the old wartime coalition turned out to be virtually the same ones addressed by Stalin, Churchill, and Roosevelt: the freedom of Eastern Europe, the unification of Germany and a German peace treaty, the withdrawal of the Red Army, and a security system to contain Germany's revival. It seemed as if Bush and Gorbachev would succeed where Stalin, Roosevelt, and Churchill had failed. The reason was simple. The old cold war order in Europe created by Stalin and preserved by Khrushchev and Brezhnev was gone. In a period of stunning surprises nothing could sum up the new era better than the dramatic television pictures of the opening of the Berlin Wall.

Yet perhaps the most telling symbol was the picture, a year earlier, of Ronald Reagan, Mikhail Gorbachev, and George Bush standing together with the Statue of Liberty in the background. It was, after all, the spirit of liberty that had always haunted the Soviet empire and in the end had forced Mikhail Gorbachev to sue for peace.

16

EPILOGUE

The United States and its allies won the cold war for two reasons. First, the United States formed a new coalition after the war with its allies, Britain and France, and eventually with the defeated powers—Germany, Japan, and Italy. This new coalition proved far too strong for the Soviet Union, especially after the defection of communist China. The Soviet Union exhausted itself first in trying to prevent this coalescence and then in trying to compete with it. The economic burden of expanding abroad, sustaining an empire, and maintaining a huge military establishment was crushing. Gradually, as the other instruments of Soviet policy faltered, the military dimension grew in importance, for it still defined the USSR as a superpower. By the time Brezhnev died, however, the economy of the Soviet Union was bankrupt, its ideology was sterile, and its policies were impotent. Even nuclear weapons gained the Soviet Union little, especially when confronted by the prospect of a new and dangerous arms race. In the end the Soviet system was profoundly weakened by all of these strains and the Bolshevik revolution itself was seriously threatened.

The United States did not win the cold war only because the Soviet Union was contained. The policy of containment had indeed triumphed in Europe, but it had failed significantly in Asia. Nor did it prevent the expansion of Soviet power. Brezhnev's successors might have tried to continue the cold war, but the system on which the strategy depended was failing not only because it was contained by the United States. The Soviet system failed because it was inherently and fatally flawed.

Gorbachev recognized the threat to the Soviet Union and acted to save the Bolshevik revolution by radical economic reforms, political liberalization, and, finally, a new foreign policy. He thus became the crucial figure in ending the cold war. How successful he will be in curing an ailing system is the central question of the post-cold-war era.

It is ironic that the communist system failed in the very arenas in which it was supposedly destined by history to triumph: as a political philosophy for organizing power, it exalted the state at the expense of freedom and the individual; as an economic system, it centralized authority at the cost of incentives and efficiency. It preached social equality but supplied an oppressive and rigid hierarchy. Finally, the Soviet system could not be transplanted whether in Asia or in the older cultures of Eastern and Central Europe.

There was a period in the 1960s when the Soviet leaders hoped to win the cold war by outflanking the United States in the third world, where communism still held some attraction. By the 1980s, however, the fundamental communist ideology appealed to few countries. Cuba and Nicaragua had become relics. Virtually no one wanted to adopt or imitate the Soviet economic model. In those areas of Europe where the system had been imposed for forty years a rebellion finally broke through and swept away the entire old guard. This accumulation of failures is the second reason why the United States and its allies were able to prevail in the cold war. The strength of the western powers, reinforced by the appeal of freedom and buttressed by the superiority of the noncommunist economies, all combined to defeat the communist system.

Its fatal weaknesses are now being examined and explained by Soviet ideologues. It has been too easy to blame Stalin or the imperialists. Now at long last Soviet scholars and political leaders are beginning to question Leninism. Put in simplest terms, some are concluding that Lenin was a poor judge of human aspirations. As one scholar put it: Marxist theory was "in conflict with life." What several generations of western orators had proclaimed all along turned out to be quite right: freedom was stronger.

Nationalism also played a strong part, especially in recent years.

Whether in China or in Europe, a national consciousness could not be suppressed. Fear of the Soviet Union contained national aspirations in Eastern Europe and Germany, but the long-term effect was to provoke an even greater nationalism, a virulent anticommunist revolution, and an irresistible desire for independence. The Europe of 1989 evoked memories of 1848 and even of 1789.

The Soviet leaders could not combat this revival of nationalism, if only because inside the Soviet Union itself the national virus proved to have been only dormant. As the policies of perestroika and glasnost took hold, the various non-Russian nationalities (145 million) began to assert themselves, and Great Russian nationalism also revived, first as a defensive reaction, then with more aggressive and offensive overtones—an ominous portent of further conflict in the USSR.

═══

Even though the cold war has ended, negotiating a final peace will not be an easy task. Some of the issues have simply disappeared. There is no need to resolve the ideological contest. The West won that long ago. The economic competition was also won years ago, although integrating the sick economy of the Soviet Union into a healthy international community is a monumental challenge. Two core political issues that remain—the future of Eastern Europe and the position of Germany—will not simply fade away, for they will determine Europe's immediate future.

In the Soviet empire in Eastern Europe, there has already been an amazing transition toward autonomy and democratic revolution everywhere behind the old Iron Curtain. How far can Moscow go in tolerating liberties on its borders that are denied inside the Union of Soviet Socialist Republics? Will Poland or Hungary be the model for the Soviet Union in the 1990s?

Is the Bolshevik Revolution truly over? But if so, what of Soviet expansion? Can any leader in Moscow, communist or czar, preside over the dismantling of an empire acquired over more than two centuries of conquest? Will these new, liberated countries of Eastern Europe form a neutral belt, a new *cordon sanitaire* separating Russia from the West, or will they inevitably gravitate toward Western Europe? Would Moscow tolerate a buffer zone without adequate security guarantees? How can the West negotiate such guarantees without engaging in a new Yalta? Yet if there is no understanding among the Great Powers, can matters be allowed to take their course without courting new risks? Romania was a terrifying reminder of the dangers. In the end, Moscow cannot be excluded from Europe, but how can Europe be free if it includes the power of the Soviet Union? A new balance of power seems to be the answer.

A tentative outline of this new balance has begun to emerge.

By the spring of 1990, the two superpowers had apparently reached some fundamental understandings: namely, that both want to preserve a high degree of political stability in Europe at a time of great upheaval. Gorbachev encouraged the revolutions in Central and Eastern Europe, but tried to set limits that would not threaten Soviet security, and he made this clear in private communications to George Bush. The president, in turn, agreed to respect those limits and not press the revolution beyond its natural rhythm. Both agreed that the formal structure of the two alliances, NATO and the Warsaw Pact, ought to be maintained for some time, though the character of both alliances might become more political, while the German question would be left to "history." They also agreed that some level of their armed forces would be maintained in Europe in the transition period.

In effect, each side tried to allay the apprehensions of the other on the future of Europe. During the Romanian crisis, both sides seemed to be signaling a mutual desire that the revolt succeed; the United States went so far as to accept the possibility of a Warsaw Pact intervention. And the secretary of state made a significant gesture of reassurance when he went to Berlin and met with the new communist government, after the four ambassadors had met in Berlin, for the first time since 1971, to underline their continuing responsibility for the future of Germany. Thus, in words and deeds the superpowers began to define the post-cold-war order, but events were moving rapidly.

Gorbachev's role has become more important. At this first post-cold-war summit (at Malta) he seemed more subdued, which may be under-standable. It cannot be easy to preside over the dismantling of an empire, or to make the symbolic journey to Canossa to meet a former Polish parish priest in the Vatican. (Was Gorbachev thinking of Stalin's cynical ques-tion: how many divisions does the Pope have?) In any case, while in Rome Gorbachev added an amazing new dimension to perestroika by virtually agreeing to permit free religion inside the USSR.

The period of hesitation in Washington over Gorbachev's durability and the desirability of dealing with him ended in Malta. George Bush went further than any of his predecessors when he identified himself as an advocate of perestroika. No American leader has singled out an internal Soviet program for such specific endorsement. Moreover, he committed the United States to a lengthy process of bringing the Soviet Union into the world economy.

Even the modalities of the post-cold-war world are different. At Malta the two leaders held lengthy sessions without signing any concrete agree-ments or issuing the usual ponderous but easily forgettable communiqué. The summit occurred while the United States was casually intervening in the internal affairs of the Philippines and the entire East German politburo was resigning in disgrace. A new world, indeed. Summits were becoming easier and less pretentious as the relationship between the two strongest nuclear powers eased.

The substantive test, however, will be whether the two sides can fulfill an ambitious new agenda: a new trade agreement, four or five arms control agreements, one or two European summit conferences, and at least one more superpower summit in the United States. In 1990, this agenda had become an almost routine recitation, but if its content is realized it will be a sea change.

At the core of any new security system, however, is the insistent German question. No European state truly wants a powerful Germany. Both Moscow and Washington made this clear, but Germany will be united. As Soviet power withdraws from Eastern Europe, the entire area changes its alignment. It is difficult to believe, however, that Moscow will ever agree to a united Germany that remains a member of NATO, especially if American troops are stationed there. But even this is no longer ruled out. Will a united Germany mean the end of the European dream of Monnet, and perhaps the end of NATO as well? If Germany is united once again, and Eastern Europe is free from Soviet tutelage, will Europe have returned to the very unstable situation that led to World War II? Will the end of the cold war, then, become a new prewar period?

Most of the answers depend on what happens inside the Soviet Union. Gorbachev has to drive forward an economic revolution, deter a nationalist upheaval, manage the collapse of Eastern Europe, and supervise the details of a new security relationship with the United States. His role becomes more and more critical, not only inside the Soviet Union but to the United States as well. Little wonder that Václav Havel appealed to the United States to help Gorbachev. Nevertheless, the end is not in sight for the USSR. The decline is likely to continue, perhaps even reaching the point of civil wars. Will a ruthless repression then return to establish order out of chaos? Or will the internal Soviet empire become a confederacy embracing hundreds of nationalities?

It is difficult to believe that Russia will become a second-rate power. Inevitably a Soviet-Russian state will revive, whether as a liberal social democracy, an enlightened despotism, or a brutal dictatorship. And when it does, its demands on Europe will almost certainly be similar to those posed to Churchill and Roosevelt. It will want a strong voice in Eastern Europe and Germany, and guarantees for its security on both its eastern and western fronts. It will want a large military establishment, almost certainly larger than other powers will believe justified. The new Soviet Union in whatever form will not abdicate from Russian history.

If the cold war has ended, the nuclear era has not. The two phenomena were closely related, even though nuclear weapons grew out of World War II. For most of the cold war, the nuclear competition was dominant. Even in those periods of relaxation, both sides continued to amass large nuclear arsenals, reflecting their abiding suspicions and the driving force of technology. The realization that nuclear war could not be "won," proclaimed by Reagan and Gorbachev, was a watershed. It permitted both sides to reexamine the political conflicts that originally gave rise to the nuclear competition, and it put that competition in an entirely different psychological context. Unfortunately, nuclear weapons remain and have spread. The superpowers can no longer control their existence or proliferation. The end of the cold war will allow the United States and the Soviet Union to reduce their nuclear weaponry, but the post-cold-war task of controlling the dissemination of both the weapons and the technology is quite different. It may be the most ominous cold war legacy.

And what of the United States?

No one should have any nostalgia for the cold war. It was a bitter, dangerous, and costly period in our history. We did not seek it, but it had to be fought. The end of one historical era, however, is the beginning of another. The debate has already begun over who should get the credit for ending the cold war: Reagan or Gorbachev, the liberals or conservatives, the hard line or the soft? It will be a fruitless quarrel. History will pass its judgment.

Negotiating the framework of a new order will be complicated, not only by debates over the past but by the revival of politics. Can the United States conduct an effective foreign policy without the cold war? Will Americans resist the temptation to withdraw and tend to our own domestic concerns as we did in the 1920s? Was the invasion of Panama the first post-communist skirmish, a return to the concerns of "America first"? Indeed, will the inherent isolationism of the American people reassert itself, despite the costly lessons of the last fifty years? Or will Americans be willing to bear heavy burdens to defend a new peace order, even though there is no clear and present danger?

BIBLIOGRAPHY

There is a mountain of literature on the cold war, embracing official documents, memoirs, monographs, and interpretive histories. No aspect seems to have been neglected. Unfortunately, however, the Soviet side remains much more opaque. With the advent of glasnost there has been some improvement, a trend that one hopes will continue and will help to clear up some of the remaining mysteries. Naturally, the most recent period is far less documented than the early periods. The memoirs of many in the Reagan administration will be forthcoming, but whether Mikhail Gorbachev will apply glasnost to his own period remains to be seen.

The selective bibliography that follows includes those works that seem most worthwhile. Special attention must be given to the Department of State's extensive series *U.S. Foreign Relations*; the pertinent volumes include the diplomacy of World War II through the most recent volumes, which have now reached the late years of the Eisenhower administration. Also of great value are the annual volumes published (until 1977) by the Council on Foreign Relations, entitled *The United States in World Affairs.* Since 1978, *Foreign Affairs,* the quarterly also published by the council, has published a special year-end issue, including a review of East-West relations (entitled *America and the World*).

With a few exceptions this bibliography does not include the massive periodical literature, nor does it include any works not available in English.

Acheson, Dean. *Present at the Creation.* New York, 1969.

Alliluyeva, Svetlana. *Twenty Letters to a Friend.* New York, 1967.

Ambrose, Stephen E. *Eisenhower: The President.* 2 vols. New York, 1984.

Ash, Timothy Garten. *The Uses of Adversity.* New York, 1989.

Bell, Coral. *Negotiation from Strength.* New York, 1963.

———. *The Diplomacy of Détente.* New York, 1977.

Berman, Larry. *Lyndon Johnson's War.* New York, 1989.

Beschloss, Michael R. *May-Day.* New York, 1986.

Bialer, Seweryn. *The Soviet Paradox.* New York, 1986.

Blight, James G., and Welch, David A. *On the Brink.* New York, 1989.

Bohlen, Charles. *Witness to History.* New York, 1973.

Bowker, Mike, and Williams, Phil. *Superpower Détente: A Reappraisal.* London, 1988.

Brzezinski, Zbigniew. *Power and Principle.* Rev. ed. New York, 1985.

Bullock, Alan. *Ernest Bevin: Foreign Secretary.* London, 1983.

Bundy, McGeorge. *Danger and Survival.* New York, 1988.

Churchill, Winston S. *The Second World War: Triumph and Tragedy.* New York, 1953.

Craig, Gordon, and George, Alexander. *Force and Statecraft.* New York, 1983.

Davis, Lynn Etheridge. *The Cold War Begins.* Princeton, 1974.

Dawisha, Karen. *The Kremlin and the Prague Spring.* Berkeley, Calif., 1984.

De Gaulle, Charles. *Memoirs of Hope: Renewal and Endeavor.* New York, 1971.

De Porte, A. W. *Europe Between the Superpowers.* 2nd ed. New Haven, 1986.

Diebel, Terry L., and Gaddis, John Lewis, eds. *Containment, Concept and Policy.* 2 vols. Washington, D.C., 1986.

Divine, Robert A. *Eisenhower and the Cold War.* New York, 1981.

Dockrill, Michael. *The Cold War 1945–1963*. Atlantic Highlands, N.J., 1988.

Doder, Dusko. *Shadows and Whispers*. New York, 1986.

Eisenhower, Dwight D. *Mandate for Change*. New York, 1963.

———. *Waging Peace*. New York, 1965.

Etzold, Thomas H., and Gaddis, John Lewis. *Containment: Documents on American Policy and Strategy, 1945–1950*. New York, 1978.

Djilas, Milovan. *Conversations with Stalin*. New York, 1962.

Ford, Gerald R. *A Time to Heal*. New York, 1979.

Freedman, Lawrence. *The Evolution of Nuclear Strategy*. London, 1982.

Gaddis, John Lewis. *The United States States and the Origins of the Cold War*. New York, 1972.

———. *Strategies of Containment*. New York, 1982.

Gardner, Lloyd C. *The Origins of the Cold War*. Waltham, Mass., 1970.

———. *Approaching Vietnam*. New York, 1988.

Garthoff, Raymond. *Détente and Confrontation*. Washington, D.C., 1985.

———. *Reflections on the Cuban Missile Crisis*. Rev. ed. Washington, D.C., 1989.

Gelb, Leslie, and Betts, Richard K. *The Irony of Vietnam: The System Worked*. Washington, D.C., 1979.

George, Alexander L., and Smoke, Richard. *Deterrence in American Foreign Policy: Theory and Practice*. New York, 1974.

Gilbert, Martin. *Winston S. Churchill*, vols. 6–8. Boston, 1983–88.

Gorbachev, Mikhail. *Perestroika*. New York, 1987.

Graebner, Norman, ed. *The National Security*. New York, 1986.

———. *The Cold War: Ideological Conflict or Power Struggle?* Boston, 1963.

Grosser, Alfred. *The Western Alliance*. London, 1980.

Hahn, Werner G. *Postwar Soviet Politics*. Ithaca, N.Y., 1982.

Hanrieder, Wolfram F., ed. *West German Foreign Policy, 1949–1979*. Boulder, Colo., 1980.

Harbut, Fraser J. *The Iron Curtain*. London, 1987.

Herring, George C., ed. *The Secret Diplomacy of the Vietnam War: The Negotiating Volumes of the Pentagon Papers.* Austin, Texas, 1983.

Hingley, Ronald. *Joseph Stalin, Man and Legend.* New York, 1974.

Holloway, David. "Gorbachev's New Thinking." *Foreign Affairs: America and the World 1988/89.*

Huntington, Samuel P. "Coping with the Lippmann Gap." *Foreign Affairs: America and the World 1987/88.*

Hyland, William G. *Mortal Rivals.* New York, 1987.

———, ed. *The Reagan Foreign Policy.* New York, 1987.

Johnson, Lyndon Baines. *The Vantage Point.* New York, 1971.

Johnson, Paul. *Modern Times.* New York, 1983.

Kaiser, Robert G. "The U.S.S.R. in Decline." *Foreign Affairs,* Winter 1988/89.

Kennan, George. *Memoirs 1925–1950.* Boston, 1967.

———. *Memoirs 1950–1963.* Boston, 1972.

———. "The Sources of Soviet Conduct." *Foreign Affairs,* July 1947.

Kennedy, Paul. *The Rise and Fall of the Great Powers.* New York, 1987.

Kennedy, Robert F. *Thirteen Days.* New York, 1965.

Kissinger, Henry A. *White House Years.* Boston, 1979.

———. *Years of Upheaval.* Boston, 1982.

LaFeber, Walter, ed. *The Origins of the Cold War.* New York, 1971.

Legvold, Robert. "Soviet Foreign Policy." *Foreign Affairs: America and the World 1988/89.*

Linden, Carl A. *Khrushchev and the Soviet Leadership.* Baltimore, Md., 1966.

Lippmann, Walter. *The Cold War.* Harper Torchbook ed. New York, 1972.

———. *The Coming Tests with Russia.* Boston, 1961.

Louis, W. Roger, and Bull, Hedley, eds. *The Special Relationship.* New York, 1986.

McNeal, Robert H. *Stalin.* New York, 1988.

Mandelbaum, Michael. "Ending the Cold War." *Foreign Affairs,* Spring 1989.

————, and Talbott, Strobe. *Reagan and Gorbachev.* New York, 1987.

Mastny, Vojtech. *Russia's Road to the Cold War.* New York, 1980.

Mayle, Paul D. *Eureka Summit.* Newark, N.J., 1987.

Medvedev, Roy A. *On Stalin and Stalinism.* London, 1979.

Miner, Steven Merritt. *Between Churchill and Stalin.* Chapel Hill, N.C., 1988.

Morgenthau, Hans J. *Politics in the Twentieth Century.* Chicago, 1962.

Newhouse, John. *Cold Dawn.* Pergamon-Brassey Classic Ed. New York 1989.

————. *War and Peace in the Nuclear Age.* New York, 1989.

Nisbet, Robert. *Roosevelt and Stalin.* Washington, D.C., 1988.

Nitze, Paul H. *From Hiroshima to Glasnost.* New York, 1989.

Nixon, Richard. *Memoirs.* 2 vols. Warner Books ed. New York, 1979.

Pierre, Andrew J., ed. *Nuclear Weapons in Europe.* New York, 1984.

Read, Anthony, and Fisher, David. *The Deadly Embrace.* New York, 1988.

Rhodes, James Robert. *Anthony Eden.* New York, 1987.

Rostow, W. W. *The Division of Europe After World War II: 1946.* Austin, Texas, 1981.

————. *Europe After Stalin.* Austin, Texas, 1982.

Schlesinger, Arthur M., Jr. *A Thousand Days.* Boston, 1965.

Schlesinger, James. *America at Century's End.* New York, 1989.

————. "Reykjavik and Revelations: A Turn of the Tide." *Foreign Affairs: America and the World 1986.*

Shulman, Marshall D. *Stalin's Foreign Policy Reappraised.* New York, 1969.

Smith, Gaddis. *Morality, Reason and Power.* New York, 1986.

Sorensen, Theodore C. *Kennedy.* New York, 1965.

Talbott, Strobe. *The Russians and Reagan.* New York, 1984.

————. *Endgame.* New York, 1979.

————. *Deadly Gambits.* New York, 1984.

————, trans. and ed. *Khrushchev Remembers.* Boston, 1970.

Tatu, Michel. *Power in the Kremlin.* New York, 1969.

Taubman, William. *Stalin's American Policy.* New York, 1982.

Thomas, Hugh. *Armed Truce*. New York, 1987.

Truman, Harry S. *Memoirs*. Vol. 1, *Year of Decisions*. Vol. 2, *Years of Trial and Hope*. New York, 1955, 1956.

Tucker, Robert W. "Reagan's Foreign Policy." *Foreign Affairs: America and the World 1988/89*.

Ulam, Adam B. *Expansion and Coexistence*. 2nd ed. New York, 1974.

———. *The Rivals*. New York, 1975.

———. *Dangerous Relations*. New York, 1983.

Vance, Cyrus. *Hard Choices*. New York, 1983.

White, Stephen. *The Origins of Détente*. Cambridge, England, 1985.

INDEX

not at Geneva summit, 83
and Potsdam, 68
relationship with U.S., 71–72
responsibility for war outcome in
    Europe, 38–40
return to power, 66–68
'riddle wrapped in an enigma"
    description, 18
Stalin's view of, 33
at Teheran, 49
view of Eisenhower, 76
view of involvement in Indochina,
    140
view of Stalin, 19
views on communism, 69
CIA, 57, 62, 73, 85, 116
Clay, Lucius, 47–48, 53
cold war
    beginning of, 11
    Brezhnev's role in, 8–9
    Chamberlain's role in starting,
        11–12
    formal announcement of, 41
    German future as key to, 101
    Gorbachev's role in ending, 3,
        9–10, 200
    Hitler's role in starting, 11–12, 14
    Khrushchev's role in, 7–8
    Kissinger's role in ending, 153,
        164
    Reagan's role in ending, 3, 189
    role of Helsinki Conference in
        ending, 161
    role of nuclear weapons in, 4–5,
        90
    Soviet exhaustion as factor in
        ending, 4–5, 179
    Soviet ideology as factor in
        sustaining, 182–83

Soviets admit some responsibility
    for, 185–86
Stalin's role in starting, 5–6
who won and why, 199
Cominform (Communist
    Information Bureau), 46–47
Comintern (Communist
    International), 16, 46–47
communism, 15, 184
    in Eastern Europe, 195
    failure of, 3–4, 199–200
    vs. capitalism, 182–84
communist party, 180, 192, 196
containment, 56, 92, 164, 199
correlation of forces, 59, 102
Cuba, 102, 200
Cuban missile crisis, 8, 102, 118,
    126–31, 133
    aftermath of, 131–32, 134
    Khrushchev's reasons for, 128–29
Curzon line, 26, 31, 34, 38
Czechoslovakia, 17, 30–31, 36, 38,
    47
    Charter 77 group, 160
    invited to join Marshall Plan, 45,
        47
    revolution in, 193–94, 196
    Soviet invasion of, 133, 147, 151,
        158–59, 190–91

Daoud, Mohammed, 170
de Gaulle, Charles, 18, 22, 107,
    110–11
Deng Xiao-ping, 125
détente, 8–9, 154–55, 161, 164
    ended by Afganistan invasion, 170
    in Europe, 159–60, 171–72
    revival of, by Gromyko, 177
deterrence, 92, 95, 128

INDEX

ABOUT THE AUTHOR

William G. Hyland has been the editor of the quarterly *Foreign Affairs* since 1984. Prior to his appointment he pursued a long career in both government and academic life. He entered the CIA in 1954, and subsequently served on the National Security Council staff and in the Department of State; in 1975 President Ford named him deputy assistant for national security affairs. Before assuming his duties as editor of *Foreign Affairs* he was an adjunct professor at Georgetown University and a senior associate at the Carnegie Endowment for International Peace. He is the author of *Mortal Rivals,* published in 1987, and co-author of *The Fall of Khrushchev,* published in 1968.